CHARLOTTE
BRONTË
REVISITED

CHARLOTTE
BRONTË
REVISITED

Sophie Franklin

Saraband

Published by Saraband
3 Clairmont Gardens
Glasgow, G3 7LW
www.saraband.net

ISBN: 9781912235247

Printed in the EU on paper from sustainable sources.

2 3 4 5 6 7 8 9 10

Victorian novels were commonly printed with illustrations
depicting key scenes in the narrative. Accordingly, we've
embellished this book with period images to emulate early
editions of Charlotte's works. The illustrations reproduced
in this book are from the author's own collection, or
Saraband Image Library, or else are sourced from shared-
resource and public domain collections.

CONTENTS

INTRODUCTION

There's a photo of me standing in a graveyard smiling, sur-rounded by bright green foliage and memorial stones. Trees rise above my head out of eyeshot. Behind me is the top of a grey house, with four of its symmetrical windows in view, and a little wooden gate that separates the building from the graves. There's nothing particularly notable or even eerie about the pic-ture. It's just a young woman standing at a distance from the camera in an overgrown graveyard with a house behind her.

Except it's not just that. For a lot of people – myself included – it's quite a lot more. That house behind me is Haworth Parsonage, the Yorkshire home of the Brontë family rom 1820 to 1861.

Every year, thousands of tourists make the pilgrimage up the steep, cobbled main street of Haworth to the Brontë Parsonage and Museum. Some of these people are devoted fans of Anne, Charlotte or Emily – as well as Branwell (their brother), or Patrick (their father). Some simply want to tick this destination off their touristy to-do list. Whatever their passion, people are drawn to this place, which has become so imbued with a cultural and even otherworldly significance since the mid-19th century.

It's the same impulse that took me to that spot in the graveyard, smiling for the camera. Looking again at that photo now, three years on, I'm amazed at the morbidity of it. Or maybe I mean the uncanny *absence* of morbidity, which has been replaced by a strange glee that somehow seems natural in that lush setting. What possessed me to pose for that picture? Why do so many people clamber up that hill and take photos of a house and graves, and smile while doing so? Somehow it feels too simplistic just to say 'the Brontës' and move on.

Now – after celebrating the 200th anniversary of Charlotte Brontë's birth in 1816 – feels like the right time to reflect on everything she achieved and still represents. Of course, the Yorkshire moors and the whole 'three weird sisters' thing that Ted Hughes coined in his 1979 poem, 'Haworth Parsonage', are still prominent in people's imaginations. This has shaped, and continues to shape, the reception of Anne, Emily and Charlotte's respective books; and, most dramatically, our view of their lives. But in recent years, Brontë scholars have sought to unpick the fables that surround Charlotte and her sisters, and instead offer an account of their lives stripped of mythology. In doing so, you could say the Brontës have been resurrected and reclaimed – at least in an academic and literary context. This book, however, aims to do something a little different, by revisiting Charlotte from a modern-day perspective, reconsidering why she still matters, and seeing whether there are any parallels between how we live now and how she lived then.

It begins with an overview of Charlotte's life and works. This chapter isn't necessarily designed to give my own 'version' of Charlotte, although – as with all biographical accounts – I'm sure my own prejudices will intrude somewhere. Neither is it meant as an exhaustive insight into her inner, or indeed outer, world. Think of it more as my edited highlights of her life, a series of snapshots that offer a glimpse into the various experiences that shaped her and her writing. At the end of the first chapter I have also included a chronology of the main events in Charlotte's life.

There have been numerous biographies of Charlotte, and there will surely be more to come. But this isn't necessarily a bad thing. After all, new Brontë discoveries are still emerging. In November 2015, a short story and a poem written by Charlotte in 1833 were discovered tucked away in a book owned by her mother. And, in 2017, a watercolour painting – which some believe to be of Charlotte, Anne and Emily Brontë, painted by Edwin Landseer – sold at auction or £50,000. The nature of biographies, and their cultural significance, have also changed over the years – from moralistic myth-makers to grittier, perhaps more realistic portrayals, like Sally Wainwright's popular biopic, *To Walk Invisible* (2016). Chapter Two gives a necessary primer to the previous biographies, both the sensible and the saintly, in a bid to discover the 'real Charlotte' and to ask whether there even is such a thing.

Charlotte often fuses her fictional descriptions of scenery with her characters' mental states, so that nature takes on a symbolic importance of its own. Not only is it central to her writing; it was also a big part of her life from a young age. Her youthful works are full of sweeping landscapes and dark, intense places where her characters can be and do whatever they wish. And, of course, in real life she walked for miles on the moors with her sisters, so much so that the surrounding area is now known as Brontë Country, as though each stamp of their boots was a stamp of ownership. Charlotte was also influenced by poems with an eye on nature, especially the poetry of William Wordsworth, which emphasises the connection between humanity and the surrounding empirical world. Her own nature writing combines these inspirations to become a visceral representation of both the world around her and the imagined world inside her head. Chapter Three takes a fresh look at Charlotte's nature writing and how it relates to the genre's recent upsurge.

Despite being a pro at scaring friends at school with her nightly horror stories, Charlotte was herself quite superstitious. She witnessed the deaths of Branwell, Anne and Emily within nine months of each other, and so it is little wonder she became less fond of gruesome tales. But that didn't stop her from including paranormal incidents in her writing. *Villette,* in particular, blends reality with fantasy, and its narrator, Lucy Snowe, experiences several eerie encounters of her own. And, in *Jane Eyre*, there is the infamous scene in which Jane hears Rochester's voice on the wind even though she's miles from Ferndean (it does require some suspension of disbelief).

These supernatural events tell us a lot about the psychology of the characters and the use of paranormal activities in 19th-century fiction. Nowadays, such experiences need to be explained and rationalised; otherwise, they're dismissed as silly and unconvincing. Even my comment in brackets above reveals my own feelings about these contrived antics. Really, it's time we reassessed our own perceptions of the unknown and the uncanny. By revisiting Charlotte's superstitious perspective and her supernatural descriptions, Chapter Four will do just that.

Chapter Five sets out to question the uniqueness of Charlotte's views on politics and women – and it's not always what you'd expect. Apart from *Shirley*, Charlotte's second published novel set during the Luddite rebellion, her work is not explicitly political. As she told her publisher and friend George Smith, rather self-deprecatingly, she lacked the skill to write books about 'the topics of the day'.[1] On closer inspection, and despite her protestations, Charlotte was in fact acutely political, perhaps especially from our 21st-century position. Her female narrators are complex and not always likeable individuals who walk their own path. Such characters have rightly earned Charlotte the title of 'proto-feminist'.

And then there's her Toryism. Although it isn't necessarily a focal point of her fiction, her politics did mould her outlook on society and therefore fed into her literature. Being a Tory was a bit different then from supporting the Conservative Party today, though. She may have been conservative with a small 'c' and revered the Duke of Wellington (one of the heroes of her younger writings), but her path in life was undoubtedly unconventional, so it isn't unsurprising that she is often deemed rebellious and anti-establishment.

The last chapter maps the different locations around Britain and Europe that Charlotte visited, as a means of countering the belief that the Brontës were isolated, unworldly and therefore unsophisticated. In fact, Charlotte in particular travelled quite widely, visiting the Lake District, Scotland, London and Brussels, amongst other places. Far from living an existence devoid of interaction or friendship, she was very much in the world. By tracing her numerous journeys, readers can go out and find Charlotte for themselves.

Finally, extracts from Charlotte's novels and letters have been included throughout this book, in order to place her voice at the centre of each chapter.

* * *

A few years after the smiling photo in the graveyard, I stand beside Anne Brontë's grave, which looks over Scarborough beach. My mum takes a photo of me and the two stones. This time I don't really smile. Instead, I ask myself why I did this; why I do this. Why so many of us continue to seek such strange forms of connection with long-dead authors, artists, people we never knew; and why those people still mean so much.

This book attempts in some small way to answer these questions.

ONE

THE LIFE AND WORKS
OF CHARLOTTE

THE EARLY YEARS

Charlotte was not always seen as a genius. In fact, her first school report from the Clergy Daughters' School at Cowan Bridge gave this lacklustre appraisal of her learning: 'Reads tolerably – Writes indifferently – Ciphers a little and works neatly. Knows nothing of Grammar, Geography, History or Accomplishments.' As a general remark on Charlotte's character, the report says she was '[a]ltogether clever of her age but knows nothing systematically.'[1] The fact that many of Charlotte's fellow pupils remembered her as fiercely knowledgeable – precocious enough to recite reams of poetry that her friends had never heard before – proves the common absurdity of school reports. She may have known nothing of geography or history or 'systematic' facts, but she knew plenty about literature, politics and, above all, creativity.

At this point in her life, aged eight, Charlotte was the third eldest of six siblings and had already lost her mother, Maria, to cancer in 1821. Charlotte's brief, though formative, spell at Cowan Bridge from 1824 to 1825 was the first time she had been away from home. It would prove a traumatic experience: while there, her two older sisters, Maria and Elizabeth, fell prey to tuberculosis and died shortly after returning to Haworth. The school is often cited as the inspiration for the strict bleakness of Lowood School in *Jane Eyre*:

Our clothing was insufficient to protect us from the severe cold; we had no boots, the snow got into our shoes, and melted there; our ungloved hands became numbed and covered with chilblains, as were our feet [...] Then the scanty supply of food was distressing: with the keen appetites of growing children, we had scarcely sufficient to keep alive a delicate invalid.[2]

The second school that Charlotte attended, Roe Head, was a vast improvement. While there, from 1831 to 1832, she excelled in her work, winning the silver medal for achievement three terms in a row.[3] She also made two lifelong friends: Ellen Nussey and Mary Taylor. Charlotte's letters to Ellen often form the basis of how we envisage her as a person, particularly in relation to her family, but she was in fact far more open about her intellectual activities in her epistles to Mary. Sadly, very little of what she wrote to Mary survives, meaning we may have missed out on gaining a better understanding of how Charlotte saw herself as she progressed as an artist. Regardless, her correspondences with Ellen and Mary are a testament to the power of female friendship. Their near-constant communication would sustain Charlotte through some of the darkest periods of her life.

Writing fiction was another major outlet. Since childhood, Charlotte and Branwell had been developing their own imaginary empire (see Chapter Four). Initially, this was known as the Glass Town saga, located in a largely fictionalised part of West Africa with the city of 'Verdopolis' as its capital. As the siblings' tales of conflict and lust evolved and became ever more complex, the setting was relocated to Angria, the name of which connotes the violence running through the narratives. These stories consumed Charlotte and Branwell's everyday lives, and also helped to develop their storytelling skills. The sagas began in 1826, when Patrick gave Branwell some toy soldiers; the four children named the little warriors after their own political heroes, with Charlotte choosing the Duke of Wellington and Branwell selecting Napoleon Bonaparte. This fascination with the military set the tone for much of their youthful writing, in which the characters were often in the midst of war.

By 1836, ten years later, the world of Glass Town/Angria still held sway over Charlotte's life and imagination. While working at Roe Head School, having returned as a teacher in February of that year, her reliance on the fictional realm impinged on her daily duties, as this excerpt from her journal shows:

> All this day I have been in a dream, half miserable and half ecstatic: miserable because I could not follow it out uninterruptedly; ecstatic because it shewed almost in the vivid light of reality the ongoings of the infernal world [...] Then came on me, rushing impetuously, all the mighty phantasm that we had conjured from nothing to a system strong as some religious creed. I felt as if I could have written gloriously - I longed to write. The spirit of all Verdopolis, of all the mountainous North, of all the woodland West, of all the river-watered East came crowding into my mind. If I had had time to indulge it, I felt that the vague sensations of that moment would have settled down into some narrative better at least than any thing I ever produced before. But just then a dolt came up with a lesson. I thought I should have vomited.[4]

Such a violent reaction to a child intruding on her trance-like state proves how dependent she was on writing. It gave her the opportunity to channel her passionate and intense emotions; she could give expression to thoughts she couldn't utter to anyone, even Ellen. In her Roe Head journal, she again

British and Napoleonic troops at war.

wrote: 'I'm just going to write because I cannot help it.'[5] She clearly wrestled against this irrepressible urge to put pen to paper, and it was one she often failed to resist. This impulse to write, and the interruption of her attempts, was to shape most of Charlotte's future decisions. If she couldn't control the compulsion, she could at least hold power over the content. By 1839, she decided to bid farewell to Angria and its 'burning clime', in favour of something cooler and closer to home:

> I have now written a great many books, & for a long time
> I have dwelt on the same characters & scenes & subjects
> [...] my readers have been habituated to one set of fea-
> tures, which they have seen now in profile now in full-
> face, now in outline & again in finished painting [...]
> lit with love, flushed with passion, shaded with grief,
> kindled with ecstasy, in meditation & mirth, in sorrow

& scorn & rapture [...] But we must change, for the eye is tired of the picture so oft recurring & now so familiar [...] I long to quit for a while that burning clime where we have sojourned too long. Its skies flame – the glow of sunset is always upon it. The mind would cease from excitement & turn now to a cooler region, where the dawn breaks grey and sober & the coming day for a time at least is subdued in clouds.[6]

It would be another seven years before Charlotte wrote her first novel, *The Professor*, the tale of a self-made man – far more realistic in comparison to her earlier work. In the interim, she had to focus her mind on the more pressing issue of employment.

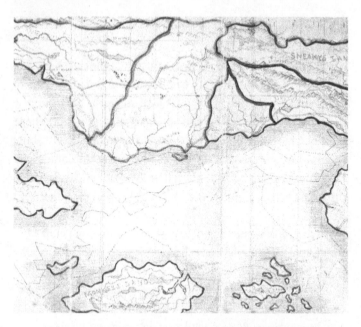

Branwell's map of Angria.

LITERARY PURSUITS

Charlotte found little pleasure in life as a governess or tutor, mostly because she was at the whim of her employers. Of all the Brontë sisters, only Anne was able to keep down a job for longer than half a year. Home had a special power over them. There, they could write, read, talk and walk together, while carrying on with their various domestic duties. Charlotte knew she must find employment, however, and her education at Cowan Bridge and Roe Head had prepared her to become a governess. She spent less than two months working for the Sidgwick family, followed by six months with the Whites at Rawdon. Neither experiences were particularly happy for Charlotte. She and Mrs Sidgwick did not see eye to eye, and in both households she felt overwhelmed by the amount of sewing she had to do, which prevented her from pursuing any work of her own. The invisibility of the governess in society was an issue she would revisit in *Jane Eyre* eight years later. While staying with the Sidgwicks, she wrote to Emily of her frustration on 8 June 1839:

> I used to think I should like to be in the stir of grand folks' society but I have had enough of it – it is dreary work to look on and listen. I see now more clearly than I have ever done before that a private governess has no existence, is not considered as a living and rational being except as connected with the wearisome duties she has to fulfil. While she is teaching the children, working for them, amusing them, it is alright. If she steals a moment for herself she is a nuisance.[7]

The problem, then, wasn't having a job in itself; it was the lack of control and the lack of time for oneself. As a governess, she had no opportunity to write in order to escape the drudgery. It is little wonder she became depressive during this time: writing was her release. So, once she'd returned home, Charlotte conceived of a plan that would enable her, Anne and Emily to remain in Haworth while still making money: they would open a school of their own.

With the financial help of their Aunt Branwell, the sisters would be able to run things their way. All they needed was a little tuition of their own. It was on this pretext, of polishing their education, that Charlotte chased the chance to move to Brussels. Her friends from Roe Head School, Mary and Martha Taylor, were already out there, so the notion of being tutored in Europe became a more tangible possibility. In her typically single-minded stubbornness, she was determined to go and, furthermore, stay there for at least a year. In the event, she stayed for two, with a short break in between when Aunt Branwell died. Although it proved to be one of the most fruitful experiences of her life, in terms of disciplining her writing practices, it was also lonely – particularly during the second year, when Emily decided to remain in Haworth with Anne, Branwell and Patrick.

After earning her spurs as an adept student, Charlotte was taken on as a teacher at the Pensionnat Héger. It was undoubtedly more favourable than her time as a governess; she had freedom and respect, and, above all, she could write. But the solitariness took her by surprise and, in October 1843, she was restless to return home:

> It is a curious position to be so utterly solitary in the midst of numbers – sometimes this solitude oppresses me to excess – one day lately I felt as if I could bear it no longer – and I went to Mde Heger and gave her notice – If it had depended on her I should certainly have soon been at liberty but Monsieur Heger – having heard of what was in

agitation – sent for me the day after – and pronounced with vehemence his decision that I should not leave – I could not at that time have persevered in my intention without exciting him to passion – so I promised to stay a while longer – how long that while will be I do not know – I should not like to return to England to do nothing – I am too old for that now – but if I could hear of a favourable occasion for commencing a school – I think I should embrace it.[8]

By early 1844, Charlotte was back in 'old England' again. She wrote to Ellen that she still hoped to set up a school, suggesting a return to brighter thoughts – or, at least, an attempt to persuade herself to push forward. This hope for the future, however, was clouded by the fact that she was still dwelling

St Michael & St Gudula Cathedral, Brussels: Charlotte visited the cathedral in 1843, while she was lonely and homesick.

on her time in Brussels and, in particular, Monsieur Héger, the husband of the school's directress: 'I think however long I live I shall not forget what the parting with Monsr Héger cost me – It grieved me so much to grieve him who has been so true and kind and disinterested a friend.'[9] Her infatuation with Monsieur Héger was to overshadow the next two years of her life, and hinder the progress of her writing. She wrote to him on 24 July 1844 about her literary aspirations and, above all, her fears. Her letters to him feel like a form of catharsis, an outpouring of her innermost secrets. This extract is tinged with a barely veiled desperation to be completely open with Héger not only about her worries for the future, but also about her feelings for him, the 'only master' she ever knew:

> I would not feel this lethargy if I could write – once I spent days, weeks, entire months writing and not all in vain because Southey, and Coleridge – two of our best writers, to whom I sent some manuscripts, were pleased to give their approbation – but at present my sight is too weak to write – if I write too much I will go blind. This weakness of sight is a terrible privation for me – without it, do you know what I would do Monsieur? – I would write a book and dedicate it to my literature master – to the only master I have ever had – to you Monsieur. I have often told you in French how much I respect you – how much I owe to your goodness, to your advice, I would like to say it once in English – that cannot be – it must not be thought of – a literary career is closed to me – that of teaching alone is open to me – it does not offer the same attractions – it does not matter, I will enter it and if I do not go far, it will not be through lack of diligence.[10]

Robert Southey.

At this stage, gaining a career as a writer remained just a dream for all three sisters. And, to top it all, the long-held plan to open a school had faltered in the face of a lack of applicants. Haworth proved too remote for pupils. This, coupled with the sudden dismissal of Branwell from his position as a tutor due to an alleged affair with his employer's wife, made the future a precarious prospect, full of uncertainty and instability both professionally and domestically.

In the autumn of 1845, however, things changed. Charlotte discovered, by chance, a notebook of verse written by Emily. That her sister wrote verse was well known to Charlotte; what she didn't know, however, was that these poems were not 'at all like the poetry women generally write'.[11] They were strange and unique. The fading fantasy of acquiring literary fame was reignited. Anne also came forward with poems that had a 'sweet sincere pathos of their own', a somewhat patronising critique.[12] Always the organiser, Charlotte persuaded her sisters that their collective poetry was worth publishing. It took a while for Emily in particular to be convinced of the scheme. She and Anne only relented when Charlotte agreed to adopt gender-neutral pseudonyms in a bid to protect themselves from public scrutiny and infamy. And so Currer, Ellis and Acton Bell entered the literary world. Within a few months, the publisher Aylott and Jones accepted the manuscript on the condition that the authors paid for the printing costs. It was a hefty sum, but Charlotte's impulse to be a published writer was too strong for the issue of money to impinge too greatly.[13] *Poems* by Currer, Ellis and Acton Bell didn't attract a great wave of attention; however, it received a handful of decent reviews, particularly in relation to Emily's contributions.

This nominal achievement spurred the sisters on to publish a piece of prose each. While Anne's *Agnes Grey* and Emily's *Wuthering Heights* found a home with the London publisher Thomas Cautley Newby (on terrible terms), Charlotte's Brussels-based *The Professor* was less lucky. Nobody wanted it. This was perhaps owing to its undercurrent of violence. There is something strangely aggressive and disturbing about its male

Anne, Charlotte, Branwell and Emily.

narrator, William Crimsworth, as though his cool surface is always ready to erupt. In the end, the novel was published posthumously. Yet, despite her being an established author by then, the book was still met with censure, particularly in regard to what her biographer, Elizabeth Gaskell, referred to as its 'coarse', blasphemous language.[14] It is still seen as an anomalous text, one with which readers and researchers are less keen to grapple.

One publisher, Smith, Elder & Co., responded to *The Professor* with a degree of enthusiasm. Beneath the strangeness of the story, they recognised the talent of its author, and asked Charlotte to send them something a little different. By this time, dismayed by the lack of interest in her first attempt, she had already begun work on *Jane Eyre*. When Smith, Elder & Co. read the manuscript, they reacted immediately. In response to their offer, Charlotte wrote a measured letter on 12 September 1847, outlining her awareness, as well as her acceptance, of their moderate terms:

> One hundred pounds is a small sum for a year's intellectual labour, nor would circumstances justify me in devoting my time and attention to literary pursuits with so narrow a prospect of advantage did I not feel convinced that in case the ultimate result of my efforts should prove more successful than you now anticipate, you would make some proportionate addition to the remuneration you at present offer. On this ground of confidence in your generosity and honour, I accept your conditions.[15]

It was lucky that she did accept their conditions – as we know, *Jane Eyre* proved a runaway hit and, over time, Charlotte made more than the promised £100 from sales. Finally, she could earn a living from her writing. She could at last call herself an author.

CHARLOTTE IN LOVE

When it came to love, however, things were a little less certain. At times, Charlotte tried to convince Ellen – and herself – that, romantically, she was under no illusions. In May 1840, at the age of just twenty-four, she wrote to her best friend that respect – not love – was the most prized form of affection in a marriage:

> Do not be over-persuaded to marry a man you can never respect – I do not say *love*, because, I think, if you can respect a person before marriage, moderate love at least will come after; and as to intense *passion*, I am convinced that that is no desirable feeling. In the first place, it seldom or never meets with a requital and, in the second place, if it did, the feeling would only be temporary: it would last the honeymoon, and then, perhaps, give place to disgust, or indifference, worse perhaps than disgust. Certainly this would be the case on the man's part; and on the woman's – God help her, if she is left to love passionately and alone.[16]

Charlotte paints herself here as a cynical, worldly-wise young woman who has love, marriage and men sussed. By this time, she was already on her second proposal, both of which she had rejected. In fact, only a year previously, Ellen Nussey's brother, Henry, had made Charlotte an offer. But, despite her later assertion that respect, and not love, was of primary importance in a marriage, she refused Henry precisely because she did not adore him. She was clearly unable to take her own sage advice:

> I thought if I were to marry so, Ellen could live with me and how happy I should be, but again I asked myself two questions – 'Do you love Henry Nussey as much as

a woman ought to love her husband? Am I the person best qualified to make him happy –?' – Alas Ellen my Conscience answered '*no*' to both these questions. I felt that though I esteemed Henry – though I had a kindly leaning towards him because he is an amiable – well-disposed man – Yet I had not, and never could have that intense attachment which would make me willing to die for him – and if I ever marry it must be in that light of adoration that I will regard my Husband…[17]

This kind of declaration is much more in line with people's perception of Charlotte as a dreamer, quixotic even. She is still painted as the diehard romantic type. After all, *Jane Eyre* is mostly about a young woman falling for an older man with an 'intense passion' that is anything but 'temporary'. Virginia Woolf, like so many before and since, made the mistake of reducing the novel to Jane's love life: 'Always to be a governess and always to be in love is a serious limitation in a world which is full, after all, of people who are neither one nor the other.'[18] Charlotte's relationship with love (and Jane's, for that matter) was far more complex than Woolf suggests.

'The Lady and the Rooks', engraving by Edward Calvert, 1829: a romanticised solitary dreamer.

John Everett Millais' engraving – an independent woman?

Some shift in outlook clearly occurred in the interim between refusing Henry Nussey and telling Ellen that love came second to respect. She'd spent just a few weeks working with the Sidgwick family as a governess. The realities of living an independent but subordinate life had perhaps mellowed her idealistic visions of marriage. But this unhappy stint of employment did not lower her standards. Having returned home from the Sidgwicks in July 1839, she received another proposal, which she also rejected.

David Pryce – or, as Charlotte referred to him, 'Mr. Price'[19] – was one of the many curates to visit Haworth over the years and, having spent an evening or two in Charlotte's company, he became enamoured of her. Despite being shy, her sharp wit and combative conversation clearly made a deep impression on him; he had barely left the parsonage, with much relief from her end, before sending a letter expressing his wish to be her husband. As she wrote to Ellen: 'I've heard of love at first sight but this beats all.'[20] For Charlotte, at this time at least, such spontaneous and unwelcome romantic gestures were greeted as a joke.

The prospect of love was often shelved in favour of Charlotte's aspirations of financial independence. Much has been made of Patrick Brontë's curate, William Weightman. He is often linked to Anne (largely due to her poem, 'I will not mourn thee, lovely one'), but Juliet Barker has contended that it is just as likely that Charlotte was in love with him.[21] He was apparently a very attractive man and she did draw his portrait, at her own suggestion. She also had a habit of mentioning him in letters unnecessarily, a clear sign that he was often on her mind. He was notoriously a bit of a flirt, too. On 14 February 1840, he sent Anne, Emily and Charlotte a Valentine each. Although this was more a case of harmless fun than a serious gesture, it was also an act of kindness. None of the sisters had received a Valentine before. The act was a sign of the man's attentiveness, and it injected some frivolity and frisson into the everyday life of the parsonage.

Charlotte did not entertain any hopes of marriage, however. She had resigned herself to a life without love, telling Ellen: 'I am tolerably well convinced that I shall never marry at all.'[22] Plus, there was work to be done. In the summer of 1841, Charlotte, Anne and Emily started to think seriously about opening their own school. Once these plans were underway, any possible interest in Weightman diminished. By 1842, Charlotte and Emily had moved to Brussels to brush up on their French and German at a school there, in preparation for their future roles as teachers. While they were away, Weightman died from cholera contracted on one of his church visits. He was only twenty-eight.

As we've already seen, Brussels was to be a defining period not only in relation to Charlotte's writing, but also her love life. It was there she met the inspiration for so many of her fictional male characters: Monsieur Héger. Charlotte fell for his masterful manner; she enjoyed being ordered about and obeying instructions. But Héger also saw qualities in Charlotte that no other person, let alone a man, had noticed before. He took her seriously as a writer, offered her constructive criticism and encouraged her talents. As an intelligent and headstrong young woman who was used to being overlooked by the opposite sex, it is little wonder she fell for a man who considered her as something far more than plain and obscure.

Having returned to Haworth for a brief time following the death of her Aunt Branwell, Charlotte went back to Brussels alone in January 1843 to take up a teaching position at the Pensionnat Héger. It was during this second trip that her regard for Héger grew into something more powerful and obsessive. As a lonely young Protestant woman in a Catholic city, Charlotte felt isolated and, so, any sign of affection or interest from Héger became a lifeline. When she considered leaving Brussels early, he convinced her to stay, a sure sign in Charlotte's mind that he wanted her around. This sense of feeling wanted, if not desired, was crucial in the development of her infatuation with him. The nature of their relationship continues to be a source of contention in Brontë studies. Although it is clear there was no affair, Charlotte's feelings for her 'master' are also indisputable. When she finally returned to Haworth at the end of 1843, having experienced extreme homesickness and depression, she wrote to Héger:

> Day and night I find neither rest nor peace – if I sleep I have tortured dreams in which I see you always severe, always gloomy and annoyed with me –
>
> Forgive me then Monsieur if I take the course of writing to you again – How can I endure life if I make no effort to alleviate my sufferings?
>
> I know that you will be impatient when you read this letter – you will say again that I am over-excited – that I

have black thoughts &c. It may be so Monsieur – I do not seek to justify myself, I submit to every kind of reproach – all that I know – is that I cannot – that I will not resign myself to losing the friendship of my master completely – I would rather undergo the greatest physical sufferings than always have my heart torn apart by bitter regrets. If my master withdraws his friendship entirely from me I will be completely without hope – if he gives me a little – very little – I will be content – happy, I will have a reason for living – for working –[23]

The rawness of Charlotte's words reveals the depth of her affection. The excessive use of dashes suggests a breathlessness that threatens to edge into frenzy. In her subsequent novels, *Jane Eyre* in particular, her heroines would also refer to their lovers as 'master', a term with which modern readers now feel uncomfortable. The schoolmaster in *Villette*, Paul Emanuel, is often seen as a fictionalised version of Héger, with his dark hair, spectacles and commanding personality. In all her leading men, there is a violent undercurrent, the possibility of an outburst both

An illustration by John Jellicoe for Villette.

passionate and harmful. Héger stamped an indelible impression over Charlotte's writing life, but it can also be said that he picked up from where her Angrian heroes left off. There is no doubt that Charlotte's romantic imagination catalysed and intensified her fixation with the schoolteacher. As we know, she was reliant on her imagination, both in childhood and adulthood, and reacted violently against any external interruptions. She could become fixated and obsessive. It is perhaps unsurprising, then, that two years after leaving Brussels, she was still writing Héger impassioned, unrestrained letters with an immediacy that implies she lived with the thought of him daily, even hourly:

> I tell you frankly ... that I have tried to forget you, for the remembrance of a person whom one believes one will never see again but whom, nevertheless, one esteems highly, harasses the spirit too much and when one has suffered this kind of anxiety for one or two years, one is ready to do anything to recover calmness. I have done everything, I have sought occupations, I have forbidden myself completely the pleasure of speaking about you

Edinburgh Old Town from Princes Street, around the time of Charlotte's daring visit with George Smith.

– even to Emily, but I cannot conquer either my regrets or my impatience – and that is humiliating – not to be master of one's own thoughts, to be slave to a regret, a memory, slave to a dominant and fixed idea which tyrannises the spirit. Why cannot I have exactly as much friendship for you as you have for me – neither more nor less? I would then be so calm, so liberated – I could keep silence for ten years without effort.[24]

Héger had stopped replying to Charlotte's increasingly desperate letters long before she stopped writing them. In fact, he tore them up. They only survive because his wife retrieved them from the bin and sewed them back together – perhaps for posterity or proof of her husband's 'innocence'.

In the grip of emotions that threatened to overwhelm her, writing once again kept Charlotte afloat. It also led to more romantic possibilities in the form of her publishers, Smith, Elder & Co. Following the publication of *Jane Eyre* in 1847, Charlotte had an intimate and often flirtatious relationship with George Smith, the handsome manager of the firm. He sent books to Haworth and she called him by his first name. And she stayed with him and his mother in London several times. They even went on an excursion to Edinburgh together, a potentially scandalous decision on Charlotte's part. For an unattached woman to go on what was effectively a holiday with a young bachelor was pretty audacious for the mid-19th century, even if his sister was present.

As a result, Ellen often teased her friend about her familiarity with George, even going so far as to insinuate that marriage was on the horizon. Unfortunately, the only prospect of a husband at this time came in the form of the publisher's clerk, James Taylor, whom Charlotte found physically repellent.[25] He proposed to her in 1851 and was, predictably, met with a refusal. As for George Smith, Charlotte's regard for him didn't weaken, but she did become more sceptical about his intentions. Believing that her looks and lack of wealth ultimately prevented George from ever proposing, she convinced herself that his friendliness was a business manoeuvre, a calculated plan to keep his author sweet. Charlotte's interpretation of George's intentions was a method of self-preservation, though it didn't prevent her from feeling disappointed when George announced his engagement to a beautiful and wealthy heiress in late 1853. If anything, his bride's beauty and money made Charlotte's situation more acute. Despite her intellect and brilliance (or perhaps because of it), she seemed destined to remain unmarried.

Although William Makepeace Thackeray was friendly with Charlotte, he gave a piercing and unkind summation of her relationship to love, and he bought wholly into the dismissive idea that her work was merely confessional, lifted entirely from her own experience:

> The poor little woman of genius! The fiery little eager brave tremulous homely-faced creature! I can read a great deal of her life as I fancy in her book, and see that rather than have fame, rather than any other earthly good or mayhap heavenly one she wants some Tomkins or another to love her and be in love with. But you see she is a little bit of a creature without a penny worth of good looks, thirty years old I should think, buried in the country, and eating up her own heart there, and no Tomkins will come. You girls with pretty faces and red boots (and what not) will get dozens of young fellows fluttering about you – whereas here is one a genius, a noble heart longing to mate itself and destined to wither away into old maidenhood with no chance to fulfil the burning desire.[26]

Charlotte may have wished desperately for love, as most of us do, but Thackeray's comments prove he had little insight into the 'creature's' inner world. Or, if he did, he had next to no empathy. There was, however, another man – not a 'Tomkins' – waiting in the wings of Charlotte's life. For several years – through the deaths of her siblings, her various publications and her flirtations with George

Thackeray.

Smith – her father's curate, Arthur Bell Nicholls, had been steadily falling in love with her. Initially, Charlotte found nothing redeeming in Arthur. When he first moved to Haworth in 1845, she deemed him narrow-minded and dull, someone not worthy of her consideration. Gradually, her feelings towards him softened and, in December 1852, she had reason to become much more aware of him. Quite unexpectedly, Arthur proposed to her one evening. In that moment, and in the months to follow, she saw a depth in him that she had never noticed before.

Her inclination towards Arthur was fuelled by her father's fierce, and rather melodramatic, opposition to the match. When he learned of Arthur's first, unsuccessful proposal to Charlotte, he became so enraged that Nicholls left Haworth for a curacy in Pontefract (although he later claimed that Patrick was not the cause). Charlotte's sense of injustice was piqued. She felt drawn to this man not only because of the intensity of his feelings for her, but because his love rendered him an outcast. Although her feelings for Arthur were less ardent, she kept in touch with him for six months and, after an issue with his replacement, he returned to his position as curate in Haworth. This opened a door of possibility, one that led to their eventual union:

Mr. N. came in Jan[uary] he was ten days in the neigh-bourhood. I saw much of him – I had stipulated with Papa for opportunity to become better acquainted – I had it and all I learnt inclined me to esteem and, if not love – at least affection – Still Papa was very – *very* hos-tile – bitterly unjust. I told Mr. Nicholls the great obsta-cles that lay in his way. He has preserved – The result of this his last visit is – that Papa's consent is gained – that his respect, I believe is won – for Mr. Nicholls has in all things proved himself disinterested and forbearing. He has shewn too that while his feelings are exquisitely keen – he can freely forgive. Certainly I must respect him – nor can I withhold from him more than mere cool respect. In fact, dear Ellen, I am engaged.[27]

Far from being happy for Charlotte, Ellen took issue with the intended marriage. Considering Arthur's attitude towards the old friends' communication, you can see Ellen's point: he deemed Charlotte's letters to be 'dangerous as lucifer matches' and asked for Ellen to burn them.[28] Charlotte found his grave expression of concern highly amusing. Thankfully, in the end, Ellen decided against burning the letters. No doubt she felt threatened by Arthur's sudden presence, hovering between her-self and her best friend. Having been such close companions for so many years, it is easy to see Ellen's side. When your ally in life's challenges, including being forever single, suddenly announces her intention to marry a man whom she used to dismiss, you might also understandably feel perplexed and selfishly peeved.

It is interesting to speculate about what might have hap-pened to her literary career if Charlotte had married earlier in life. This is especially pertinent when you consider the fact that, after her wedding, she rarely wrote, other than two chapters of a fragment entitled *Emma*. She didn't have the time.

Portrait of Arthur Bell Nicholls.

But Charlotte *was* happy – or, at least, she came to recognise her happiness over time and to accept that she had made the right decision in marrying. What she had told Ellen in 1840 had come to pass fourteen years later: respect was the foundation of her and Arthur's love. In December 1854, just three months before her death, she wrote to Ellen that Arthur was her '"dear boy" certainly – dearer now than he was six months ago'.[29] As she'd predicted, deep affection grew out of admiration. Finally, in the year before she died, Charlotte was given a taste of true contentment.

THE VALLEY OF THE SHADOW OF DEATH

Before finding such peace, however, Charlotte's home life had been overshadowed by death. Any enjoyment she might have gained from her literary success with *Jane Eyre* quickly evaporated when her three remaining siblings passed away within nine months of each other. First, Branwell died on 24

September 1848. Then Emily on 19 December 1848, almost exactly a year after the publication of *Wuthering Heights*. And on 28 May 1849 the youngest Brontë, Anne, died by the sea in Scarborough. All three contracted tuberculosis, which is now curable. Only Charlotte and her father remained in the parsonage, alongside their faithful housekeeper, Tabitha ('Tabby') Aykroyd, and Anne and Emily's dogs, Flossy and Keeper.

The death of Branwell was perhaps the least unexpected. As Charlotte wrote to her publisher, William Smith Williams, a week after her brother died:

> I do not weep from a sense of bereavement – there is no prop withdrawn, no consolation torn away, no dear companion lost – but for the wreck of talent, the ruin of promise, the untimely dreary extinction of what might have been a burning and shining light. My brother was a year my junior; I had aspirations and ambitions for him once – long ago – they have perished mournfully – nothing remains of him but a memory of errors and sufferings – There is such a bitterness of pity for his life and death – such a yearning for the emptiness of his whole existence as I cannot describe – I trust time will allay these feelings.[30]

It is a letter full of bitterness and disenchantment. Charlotte had a complicated relationship with her younger brother, exacerbated by his alcoholism, debt and entanglement with a married woman. Robert Edric's recent book, *Sanctuary*, follows the disintegration of Branwell's inner world in the final months of his life.[31] In beautifully sparse language, the novel details his collapse into death, and one of its recurring points of tension is the Brontë sisters' decision – predictably led by Charlotte – to hide their literary success from their floundering brother. In the same letter to Williams, Charlotte also confided the decision to keep their achievements a secret from Branwell:

> My unhappy brother never knew what his sisters had done in literature – he was not aware that they had ever published a line; we could not tell him of our efforts for fear of causing him too deep a pang of remorse for his own time misspent, and talents misapplied – Now he will *never* know.[32]

If you've ever visited the Haworth Parsonage, it may be difficult to imagine how anyone could be unaware of what was happening in the lives of the house's few inhabitants. But, by this time, Branwell was in the depths of addiction to alcohol and, most likely, opium. His reported lover, the married Lydia Robinson, had broken off their relationship and left him to unravel. His hopes of artistic and poetic fame had long since lost their glitter. He had fallen in with a distracting and decadent crowd, made up of some down-and-outs and other similarly ambitious but ultimately unsuccessful types. He was in severe debt and the collectors were closing in on him. All of this, coupled with his own predilection for overindulgence and escapism, plus an overwhelming sense of being a let-down to his family, made for psychological and physical chaos. He was too ill, but also (Charlotte's letter subtly suggests) too self-absorbed, to have any awareness that the three 'Bell' writers causing such a stir around the country were in fact his three sisters.

Edric's book contends that Branwell knew on some level what his sisters were doing, but was unwilling to acknowledge its truth fully both to himself and to them. This seems plausible when you consider Charlotte's attitude. In the face of such pity, such disappointment, why would – and how could – Branwell divulge his knowledge of their literary feats?

*After composing this portrait, Branwell, originally
depicted in the centre, painted over his own likeness.*

In letters, Charlotte's response to Branwell's early death was one of regret. To some, her words come across as cold and unfeeling. But she and Branwell had been literary accomplices in childhood. They had shared an intense, all-consuming fictional world, one which – according to Daphne du Maurier in her biography of Branwell – Charlotte's brother never truly left.[33] The family, and Charlotte in particular, had pinned almost impossibly grand hopes of success on him. They were all rooting for his triumph. Branwell's decline was therefore almost more heartbreaking than his death because, by then, there was nothing left of the boy with whom Charlotte had shared so much. He had eroded himself.

Just months after Branwell's untimely death, Emily's health started to weaken. Obstinately, and despite the intensifying ferocity of her cough, she refused to see a doctor and carried on with her daily domestic tasks. She was so ill that, when Charlotte presented her with a sprig of heather from her beloved moors, she did not recognise it.[34] It wasn't until the day of her death that Emily consented to a visit by Dr Wheelhouse, but by then it was too late. Almost exactly a year after the publication of *Wuthering Heights*, and less than three months after Branwell's death, Emily died at the age of thirty. A week later on Christmas Day 1848, Charlotte wrote to Williams once again, expressing her despondency and grief:

> Emily is nowhere here now – her wasted mortal remains are taken out of the house; we have laid her cherished head under the church-aisle beside my mother's my two sisters', dead long ago, and my poor hapless brother's …
>
> Well – the loss is ours – not hers, and some sad comfort I take, as I hear the wind blow and feel the cutting keenness of the frost, in knowing that the elements bring her no more suffering – their severity cannot reach her grave – her fever is quieted, her restlessness soothed, her deep, hollow cough is hushed for ever; we do not hear it in the night nor listen for it in the morning …
>
> My Father says to me almost hourly 'Charlotte, you must bear up – I shall sink if you fail me.' these words – you can conceive are a stimulus to nature. The sight too of my Sister Anne's very still but deep sorrow wakens in me such fear for her that I dare not falter. Somebody *must* cheer the rest.
>
> So I will not now ask why Emily was torn from us in the fullness of our attachment, rooted up in the prime of her own days in the promise of her powers – why her existence now lies like a field of green corn trodden down – like a tree in full bearing – struck at the root; I will only say, sweet is rest after labour and calm after tempest and repeat again and again that Emily knows that now.[35]

Emily's death brought only utter loss and a sense of deep injustice. Her demise was not quiet or resigned; she struggled for life, which only made her death all the more devastating. It is thought that she had written a second novel, as there are letters from her publisher suggesting the existence of an almost complete manuscript.[36] No such holograph has been found. It is believed that Charlotte – remembering the accusations of coarseness levelled at *Wuthering Heights* and in a bid to protect Emily's legacy – destroyed the fragments.

In the aftermath, as her letter to Williams shows, Charlotte proved her mettle by rallying her spirits for the sake of her father and remaining sister. Only in her letters to Williams did she allow her cheerful mask to slip into something closer to despair. At home, she maintained a brave face. Since the deaths of her eldest sisters, Elizabeth and Maria, twenty years before, she had been a mother-figure to her younger siblings and, to some extent, even her father. She was her family's anchor. This role was even more important in the face of Patrick and Anne falling ill from yet another bout of influenza in early January 1849, coupled with her publisher's tepid reaction to the first part of *Shirley*. The stability of home life was being dismantled by death, and now her ambitions for her second novel appeared to be faltering.

In Anne's case, this spell of the flu weakened her body, making her more susceptible to graver illnesses. Although her symptoms alleviated for a time in February, she worsened again by March. Unlike Emily, she tried to get better by seeing the doctor and using a ventilator that Ellen had kindly sent. But her cough was just like her sister's – fierce and unrelenting. Anne took control of her final few months by organising a trip to Scarborough, the seaside town that she loved. It was hoped that the sea air would do Anne's lungs some good, but the visit was also tinged with the unspoken acknowledgement that this would most likely be her last journey. While trying to ensure that the trip would go ahead, Anne wrote to Ellen in April about her hopes for the future:

> I have no horror of death … But I wish it would please God to spare me not only for Papa's and Charlotte's sakes, but because I long to do some good in the world before I leave it. I have many schemes in my head for future practise – humble and limited indeed – but still I should not like them all to come to nothing, and myself to have lived to so little purpose. But God's will be done.[37]

Anne was never able to bring her schemes to fruition. Despite initially showing her typical stubbornness by attempting to thwart Anne's planned seaside trip, Charlotte went with her sister to Scarborough on 24 May, accompanied by Ellen. By the morning of 28 May, Anne had deteriorated quickly and she died in the early afternoon with Charlotte and Ellen by her side. To prevent Patrick from having to witness another child's funeral, Anne was buried in St Mary's Church, looking out over Scarborough's sweeping beach below.

Anne's original headstone, in Scarborough.

Charlotte once again turned to William Smith Williams in this time of intense anguish. Her attempts to remain cheerful and in control over the previous nine months could no longer be sustained, and she collapsed under the strain of her loss. When she had managed to calm her nerves, she wrote to Williams, who had become her confidante and a source of comfort:

> I hardly know what I said when I wrote last – I was then feverish and exhausted – I am now better and – I believe – quite calm.
>
> You have been informed of my dear Sister Anne's death – let me now add that she died without severe struggle – resigned – trusting in God – thankful for release from a suffering life – deeply assured that a better existence lay before her – She believed – she hoped, and declared her belief and hope with her last breath. – Her quiet – Christian death did not rend my heart as Emily's stern, simple, undemonstrative end did – I let Anne go to God and felt He had a right to her   I could hardly let Emily go – I wanted to hold her back then – and I want her back now – Anne, from childhood seemed preparing for an early death – Emily's spirit seemed strong enough to bear her to fulness of years – They are both gone – and so is poor Branwell – and Papa has now me only – the weakest – puniest – least promising of his six children – Consumption has taken the whole five.[38]

This was a desolate, lonely time for Charlotte. She remained on the coast with Ellen for a few weeks to convalesce and regain strength, putting off the return home at the insistence of Patrick. When she arrived back at the parsonage, she spent her evenings in solitude in the dining room. The three sisters used to circle the dining table reciting their works in progress, giving feedback and encouragement. Charlotte continued the tradition. Only, now, she was the only one circling the room.

Her writing, then, became her constant and trusted companion. It kept her going through the darkest time, what she called the 'valley of the shadow of death' in her novel *Shirley*, which she finished in the months following Anne's death.[39] Throughout all the painful episodes of her life, writing had always emerged as a salvation, sustaining her like blood – this time, it was no different.

'FOR EVER KNOWN'

The last years of Charlotte's life saw the realisation of some of her early dreams. She had secured literary renown. As we know, she would go on to be 'for ever known', fulfilling the wish she had expressed to the Poet Laureate Robert Southey in 1837 as a twenty-year-old.[40] Her second published novel, *Shirley*, was a controversial follow-up to *Jane Eyre*, not least because it was not in the intimate first-person voice. Reviewers were quick to point out the novel's defects: its meandering, and at times plodding, plot was chief amongst the criticism. They were also somehow able to guess the true gender of 'Currer Bell', with one review even identifying the author as a Yorkshire woman with experience as a governess.[41] Such pinpointed speculation meant Charlotte's real identity was finally out.

This gave her a degree of freedom, as well as the eminence she secretly desired. Now that she was no longer anonymous, she felt able to accept invitations from her publisher to visit London where she met her hero, William Makepeace Thackeray. In her unworldliness, she had caused a stir by dedicating the second edition of *Jane Eyre* to Thackeray. Unbeknownst to Charlotte, he had a wife who was mentally ill, and critics therefore drew unfavourable and cruel comparisons between her

Bertha Mason's suicide.

and the character of Bertha Mason, 'the mad woman in the attic'. Charlotte was understandably mortified by the insinuations that she was Thackeray's governess and that this was a strange form of revenge against the 'mad' Mrs Thackeray.

While this anecdote was by no means typical of Charlotte's venture into city life, it does reveal her naivety and heightens the feeling that she was set apart from literary circles of the time. This was exacerbated by her apparently disappointing appearance and minimal bantering skills: when she visited the Thackeray family, her blatant and ill-fitting hairpiece drew sniggers from the guests; and she often replied to (admittedly vacuous) questions with monosyllabic answers.[42] She was nothing like Becky Sharp, the anti-heroine of Thackeray's *Vanity Fair*. Like many highly intelligent introverts, it took a long time to break beneath Charlotte's reserved carapace to see a more engaging side of her.

Despite this, she did make friends, particularly with Elizabeth Gaskell, and also the writer and social theorist Harriet Martineau (until an argument over the apparent over-emphasis of love in *Villette*). After Charlotte's death, her father would commission Gaskell to write his daughter's biography, believing her reputation to be safe in such trusted hands. She did not disappoint; *The Life of Charlotte Brontë* remains one of the most successful and influential biographies of that genre. Its depiction of Charlotte as a martyr, someone who sacrificed her own happiness for others, continues to shape how we remember Charlotte Brontë to this day.[43]

In 1853, *Villette* saw Charlotte return to the first-person narrative, and it is arguably the unsung masterpiece of her oeuvre. She came full circle with the book, going back to Brussels and revisiting her all-consuming attachment to Monsieur Héger. When you read *Villette*, you can feel Charlotte pouring both her life's anguish and her masterful writing style into its pure, visceral prose. Its ambiguous ending, in which Paul Emanuel may or may not drown, is emblematic of Charlotte's hard-won confidence in her writing abilities. She was willing to toy with the reader, refusing to commit to a neat and ultimately unrealistic happy ending. Of the novel's close, she told George Smith:

> With regard to that momentous point – M. Paul's fate – in case any one in future should request to be enlightened thereon – they may be told that it was designed that every reader should settle the catastrophe for himself, according to the quality of his disposition [...] Drowning and Matrimony are the fearful alternatives. The Merciful [...] will of course choose the former and milder doom – drown him to put him out of pain. The cruel-hearted will on the contrary pitilessly impale him on the second

horn of the dilemma – marrying him without ruth or
compunction to that – person – that – that – individual
– 'Lucy Snowe'.[44]

There was to be no final 'Reader, I married him' moment for
her last heroine.

Charlotte died on 31 March 1855, less than a month before
her thirty-ninth birthday. She was pregnant, and her small
body was unable to cope with the hyperemesis gravidarum
(extreme vomiting in pregnancy) from which she suffered.
She was buried alongside her mother, aunt and four siblings
in the family vault beneath Haworth Church. She left behind
her father, who lived until the grand age of eighty-four, and
her husband Arthur, who moved back to Ireland after Patrick's
death in 1861.

But, beyond her family, she also left a legacy that continues
to excite and challenge readers, one that has been rightly revit-
alised and reconsidered in almost every era since her death.
Charlotte led a real life in that it was full of suffering and success, the highs and lows of all humans. She had felt ugly, alone
and unloved; she frequently found herself pursuing men unre-
quitedly; worst of all, she watched her family members die one
by one. Her path to literary success and domestic satisfaction
with Arthur was not smooth. Yet, despite her ordinariness in
this respect, she was a remarkable woman and writer, willing
to face whatever life threw her way. As ever, her philosophy
can be gleaned from a letter to Ellen, written in the wake of her
siblings' deaths: 'but Life is a battle May we all be enabled to
fight it well [sic]'.[45] She may have been no martyr, but she was a
warrior until the very end.

CHRONOLOGY OF
CHARLOTTE'S LIFE & WORKS

1816   Charlotte Brontë is born on 21 April. She is the third child of the Reverend Patrick Brontë and Maria Branwell, and has two elder sisters, Maria and Elizabeth.

1817   Patrick Branwell Brontë is born on 26 June.

1818   Emily Jane Brontë is born on 30 July.

1820   Anne Brontë is born on 17 January.
The family moves to Haworth Parsonage in April of this year.

1821   Charlotte's mother, Maria Brontë, dies from cancer on 15 September.

1824   Maria and Elizabeth attend the Clergy Daughters' School at Cowan Bridge from late July. Charlotte follows them in August, and Emily goes in November.

1825   Maria returns home from Cowan Bridge with tuberculosis on 14 February. She dies on 6 May.
Elizabeth is also sent home ill on 31 May. Charlotte and Emily leave the next day.
Elizabeth dies on 15 June.

1826   Branwell receives the toy soldiers that spark the siblings' documentation of their rich fictional worlds.
All the Brontë children remain at Haworth until 1830, where they are looked after by their aunt, and indulge in their imaginary and literary realms.

1831   On 17 January, Charlotte goes to school at Roe Head, under the direction of Margaret Wooler. While there, she befriends Ellen Nussey and Mary Taylor, and they become lifelong friends.

1832   Charlotte leaves Roe Head in June.

1833   Charlotte writes prolifically during this period, including the short stories 'Something About Arthur', 'Green Dwarf' and 'The Foundling'.

1835   In July, Charlotte returns to Roe Head as a teacher.

1836   At the end of the year, Charlotte contacts the Poet Laureate Robert Southey, who replies to her letter in early 1837.

1838   In December, Charlotte leaves her role as teacher at Roe Head.

1839   In March, Charlotte refuses an offer of marriage from Henry Nussey (Ellen's brother).
In May, she begins her post as governess to the Sidgwick family, which she leaves after less than two months.
In the summer, she once again refuses a proposal, this time from David Pryce.

1841   In March, Charlotte starts her six-month stint as governess to the White family at Upperwood House, Rawdon.

1842   In February, Charlotte travels to Brussels with Emily to enrol at the Pensionnat Héger, school for girls. Both undertake language lessons as part of their plan to found their own school in Yorkshire.

On 29 October, their Aunt Branwell dies and both sisters return home for the funeral in November.

1843 Charlotte goes back to Brussels as a teacher, this time without Emily as company. As a result, and intensified by her burgeoning infatuation with Monsieur Héger, she suffers from loneliness and depression.

1844 Charlotte returns home from Brussels in January and starts to write heartfelt letters to Héger. Preparations for the sisters' Yorkshire school flounder, as prospective pupils deem Haworth too remote.

1845 Charlotte discovers a journal full of Emily's poetry and convinces her sisters to seek publication for their poems under pseudonyms.

1846 Currer, Ellis and Acton Bell (the Brontë sisters' chosen *noms de plume*) publish – and pay for – an anthology of poetry.

1847 In October, Charlotte's *Jane Eyre* is published and praised widely in the press. This followed the unfortunate and repeated rejection of her first novel, *The Professor*.
In December, Emily's *Wuthering Heights* and Anne's *Agnes Grey* are published in a single edition.

1848 In June, Anne's *The Tenant of Wildfell Hall* is published.
Branwell dies on 24 September.
Emily dies on 19 December.

1849 Anne dies at Scarborough on 28 May.
Charlotte's second novel, *Shirley*, is published in October.

At the end of the year, she visits London and meets William Thackeray and Harriet Martineau for the first time.

1850 Charlotte meets Elizabeth Gaskell in August while visiting mutual friends in the Lake District.

1851 Charlotte visits London and attends the Great Exhibition five times.
In April, James Taylor, her publisher's clerk, proposes to Charlotte. She declines the offer.

1852 Charlotte completes a draft of the first volume of *Villette* in March.
In December, Arthur Bell Nicholls, her father's curate, asks Charlotte to marry him. Her father resists the match.

1853 *Villette* is published at the end of January.

1854 On 29 June, Charlotte marries Arthur Bell Nicholls. They honeymoon in Ireland where Charlotte meets Arthur's family.

1855 Charlotte dies on 31 March.

1857 *The Professor* is published posthumously.
Elizabeth Gaskell's biography, *The Life of Charlotte Brontë*, is published.

1861 Patrick dies on 7 June. Arthur returns to his native Ireland.

TWO

CHARLOTTE'S
AFTERLIVES

Some claim that this was painted by Edwin Landseer, who was connected to the Brontës via the Nussey family. There are several 'portraits' for which the identity of the sitters or artist is unconfirmed.

There are many versions of Charlotte Brontë. Whether or not you read and enjoy her novels, most people will have some opinion or vision of her as an author and as a woman. Often this involves pitting her against her sisters and fellow writers, Anne and Emily. I'm asked frequently which Brontë is my 'favourite', as though they can be ranked by talent and approachableness. Say 'Anne', and you receive a puzzled but intrigued look of approbation, as though you have revealed yourself to be a deeply mysterious and unconventional individual. Name 'Charlotte', however, and you are often – in my experience – met with a slight smirk. *Charlotte.* Of course. The obvious option.

And, sometimes, she is the unpopular one. Those who cite Emily or Anne as their 'favourite Brontë' can be defensive about Charlotte's position as (arguably) the best-known, and certainly the most vocal, sister. There hangs over Charlotte's legacy the strong possibility that she destroyed the manu-script of Emily's second novel. At the very least, she undoubt-edly altered and censored Emily's poetry and other writing – at times removing and then including whole stanzas of her own composition, thereby changing the whole meaning of the poem.

In her 1850 preface to *Wuthering Heights*, Charlotte was the first to present Emily as a recluse, as someone more at home on the moors than in the company of people. Her contention that Emily 'did not know what she had done' when she cre-ated characters like Heathcliff paved the way to the prevalent vision of her sister as an ethereal and disembodied genius, but also ultimately as some kind of woman-child who could not control her own violent literary powers.[1] As for Anne's work, Charlotte wrote publicly that *The Tenant of Wildfell Hall* was 'an entire mistake'.[2] This more calculated, even manipulative side to Charlotte rarely wins her any admirers.

And nor should it. *My* Charlotte Brontë is combative and fierce, prone to prickliness and often on the defensive. She is also violently loyal and eminently lovable. When you read her letters, their warmth is still palpable two centuries on. Like so many Brontë readers, I think Charlotte and I could have been good friends. But it feels wrong – almost like a betrayal – to admit that, especially as I now read her books with such an academically critical eye. It also feels wrong because I hate to reduce Charlotte to the kind of person with whom you want to be friends. It's such a safe and comforting term, one that fails to accommodate her powerful intellect or her often acerbic wit. It's a bit like a pat on the head.

While there is also a pathos to my version of Charlotte, she is never a victim, never someone to be pitied. Perhaps I'm conflating Charlotte with her most famous heroine, Jane Eyre, by painting her as a fighter who never gives up. But I don't think it is wrong to see some of Jane in Charlotte – after all, she created that character. And, in a way, *Jane Eyre* and its success created Charlotte Brontë, the best-selling author. I don't mean to idealise her, any more than I wish to make her seem ordinary. For she was, as we can see throughout this book, both flawed and brilliant.

This chapter gives an overview of the various biographies and interpretations of her life and works over the last 160-odd years, tracing the shifting approaches to her as a writer and woman. Biographers – just like any 'ordinary fan' of Charlotte and her writing – read their own interests and priorities into her experiences. We all believe we are trying to find a coherent and 'real' narrative of her identity, but it is always one that fits within our own ideas of her. What emerge, in fact, are versions of ourselves refracted through the prism of Charlotte's life.

THE BIOGRAPHERS

Early Lives

When it comes to tracing the development of Charlotte's biographies, it's necessary to begin with Charlotte herself. As Barbara Mitchell, and more recently Lucasta Miller, have identified,[3] the first shaping of the Brontës' legacy occurred in Charlotte's 'Biographical Notice of Ellis and Acton Bell' in the 1850 edition of *Wuthering Heights* and *Agnes Grey*.

Although she was not technically writing about her own life, she uses the pronoun 'we', thereby including herself in the description and justification of her sisters' lives and works. She believes it is her 'duty to explain briefly the origin and author-ship of the books written by Currer, Ellis, and Acton Bell'.[4] In revealing aspects of the everyday lives of her sisters, Charlotte is also divulging details about her own life:

Resident in a remote district where education had made little progress, and where, consequently, there was no inducement to seek social intercourse beyond our own domestic circle, we were wholly dependent on ourselves and each other, on books and study, for the enjoyments and occupations of life. The highest stimulus, as well as the liveliest pleasure we had known from childhood upwards, lay in attempts at literary composition [...]⁵

The image of the Brontës as the 'three weird sisters' has its roots in this brief paragraph, sparking the basis of what Lucasta Miller terms the 'Brontë myth'.⁶ Charlotte's biographical notice, then, was an extraordinarily prescient attempt to control the future narrative and reputation not only of her sisters, but also herself. If she was to be 'for ever known', she wanted to steer her legacy in the right direction. In true authorial style, Charlotte took command of her own story from the beginning.

Despite the dissolution of their friendship, Harriet Martineau wrote, in 1855, a warm obituary for Charlotte, which also shaped the perception of the writer. Her posthumous memorial is sensational at best, inaccurate at worst:

'Currer Bell' is dead! The early death of the large family of whom she was the sole survivor prepared all who knew the circumstances to expect the loss of this gifted creature at any time: but not the less deep will be the grief of society that her genius will yield us nothing more [...] We all remember how long it was before we could learn who wrote [*Jane Eyre*], and any particulars of the writer, when the name was revealed. She was living among the wild Yorkshire hills, with a father who was too much absorbed in his studies to notice her occupations, in a place where newspapers were never seen (or where she never saw any), and in a house where the servants knew nothing about books, manuscripts, proofs or the post. When she told her secret to her father, she carried her book in one hand, and an adverse review in the other, to save his simple and unworldly mind from rash expectations of a fame and fortune which she was determined should never be the aims of her life.[7]

As subsequent books – such as Juliet Barker's immense *The Brontës* and Lyndall Gordon's *Charlotte Brontë: A Passionate Life* – have proven, this image of the family as reclusive and of Charlotte as unambitious is overblown. As we shall see in the following chapters, the idea of Haworth as some uncivilised hicksville that never saw newspapers is laughable. Her father kept several papers in the house on a weekly, if not daily, basis and Charlotte read them voraciously. But the depiction of Charlotte as dutiful and passive, the 'perfect household image', would be harder to unstick.[8]

In a way, Elizabeth Gaskell's *The Life of Charlotte Brontë* was a continuation of Charlotte's own biographical self-fashioning and Harriet Martineau's obituary. In an attempt to counter accusations of immorality and coarseness levelled against her friend's novels, Gaskell decided to go on the defensive and present Charlotte in saint-like terms. This approach wasn't too dissimilar to the method Charlotte used in her 'Biographical Notice of Ellis and Acton Bell', in which she tried to excuse and justify the more shocking aspects of her sisters' books. In this way, the first Brontë biographies were a form of resistance against hostile reviewers and self-defence against detractors.

Gaskell and Charlotte became friendly in the last few years of Charlotte's life, visiting each other, meeting their respective families, and sharing confidences. As we have already seen in Chapter One, her version of Charlotte is still a major influence on how we perceive Brontë and her family today. In particular, biographers continue to contend with Gaskell's characterisation of Patrick Brontë. He is painted as a violent eccentric who, instead of talking through his problems, would work off 'his volcanic wrath by firing pistols out of the back-door in rapid succession'.[9] Having provided this strange story, amongst others, Gaskell then refuses to analyse the incident, writing:

> I do not pretend to be able to harmonize points of character, and account for them, and bring them all into one consistent and intelligible whole. The family with whom I have now to do shot their roots down deeper than I can penetrate. I cannot measure them, much less is it for me to judge them. I have named these instances of eccentricity in the father because I hold the knowledge of them to be necessary for a right understanding of the life of his daughter.[10]

Elizabeth Gaskell as a young woman.

This suggests that she had no hidden agenda, that she was simply presenting the basic facts of Charlotte's life, leaving the reader to judge for themselves: 'I cannot measure or judge of such a character as hers. I cannot map out vices, and virtues, and debateable land'.[11] But the judgemental reader was always on Gaskell's mind, as proven by the final words of the biography:

> But I turn from the critical, unsympathetic public, – inclined to judge harshly because they have only seen superficially and not thought deeply. I appeal to that larger and more solemn public, who know how to look with tender humility at faults and errors; and how to admire generously extraordinary genius, and how to reverence with warm, full hearts all noble virtue. To that Public I commit the memory of Charlotte Brontë.[12]

The Charlotte whom Gaskell 'committed' to the public's collective memory was the woman, not the writer. Any focus on her literary aspirations and achievements were subsumed into the portrayal of Charlotte as a domestic angel of the house. She was not a virago; she was a stoic sufferer, one whom 'civilised' readers could identify with and pity.

A later portrait of Elizabeth Gaskell.

In this sense, Gaskell's version of Charlotte was calculated to fit with the contemporary stereotype of women as submissive and dutiful, never straying beyond the bounds of feminine propriety. By fixing Charlotte into this mould, Gaskell thought she was doing her friend a favour. And, to an extent, she was also maintaining the identity Charlotte had herself projected in the last years of her life.

This emphasis on Charlotte's persona often overshadowed her accomplishments as a novelist. In the 100 years after the impact of Gaskell's biography, there were major developments in the exploration of Charlotte's youthful writing – thanks to the pioneering work of Fannie E. Ratchford – and the dissemination of her letters.[13] Despite this, there was no meaningful overlap between Charlotte-the-writer and Charlotte-the-woman. These remained distinct identities which researchers and biographers felt unable to entwine.

Published in 1967, Winifred Gérin's enduringly acclaimed *Charlotte Brontë: The Evolution of Genius* was, in her own words, the first biography that attempted to present Charlotte 'whole'.[14] Before, biographers had focused on only specific aspects of Charlotte's life; alternatively, they had set out with an agenda in mind. Of course, Gérin had her own angle, as all life writers do. After all, even the notion that the essence of a person's life can be contained in one book is debatable. As Virginia Woolf suggested in her essay 'The Art of Biography' (1939), keeping to the facts is dull, but roaming from reality is dangerous. The biographer, then, is stuck between the two. Woolf did allow that, in order for a biography to be successful, they must be willing to accept and represent the various, often contradictory, faces worn by their object of interest.[15]

Regardless of this, Gérin's book was more thorough and complete than previous efforts. Several subsequent biographers and researchers have conceded that, in many respects,

Gérin's offering can be seen as the last word on Charlotte. This is particularly true in relation to her treatment of Charlotte's complicated relationship with her brother Branwell, as well as her analysis of the Monsieur Héger affair (or non-affair) in Brussels. But this didn't prevent Barbara Hardy from claiming that the book was not critical or searching enough in its exploration of Charlotte's literature.[16] The marrying of Charlotte's two public selves – the saint and the author – was still to be done. The search for her 'true self' continued.

How We See Charlotte Now

Biographies are often responses to and even retaliations against those that have appeared before. Each time a new Brontë biography comes out, then, it must position itself in relation to previous attempts – and it must eventually contend with the spectre of Gaskell. It has to unsettle long-held perceptions, sometimes even aggressively repudiating older accounts in favour of an updated, more contemporary life story. Since Charlotte's death in 1855 over 160 years ago, there have been numerous readings and discoveries, followed by countless re-readings and re-discoveries. These have accumulated and form the basis of our vision of Charlotte today.

So, how do we see her now? Obviously, this book gives an insight into how Charlotte's writing reflects aspects of our own contemporary moment. But, in recent years, there have been several innovative approaches to her life and works that have refashioned, once more, the Charlotte we (think we) know.

The subtitle of Rebecca Fraser's 1988 biography of Charlotte, *A Writer's Life*, promised to put Brontë's literary persona first. Its premise, as well as Lyndall Gordon's later offering, *Charlotte Brontë: A Passionate Life* (1994), stemmed from the surge in feminist critique and scholarship. Fraser's biography was responding to the second-wave feminist revolution of the '70s

'How dare I, Mrs Reed? It's the truth!' Some readers project much about Charlotte from her characters – particularly Jane Eyre.

and '80s. For her, Charlotte was unequivocally and passionately feminist in her beliefs and in the way she lived. Such a view of Charlotte has, as Fraser herself later noted, become mainstream and increasingly associated with the subject matter of her novels. Although portraying Charlotte as an indisputable proto-feminist figure is not necessarily inaccurate, it does come with some qualification, which you can read more of in Chapter Five. Regardless, this feminist interpretation of Charlotte was a new, and necessary, frontier for Brontë biographers.

Fraser also wanted to place Charlotte within her own contemporary context, to try to recapture how her generation saw and reacted to her work and life. And, in keeping with her feminist credentials, she similarly wished to present the contradictory sides of her subject, just as Virginia Woolf had advised.

Fraser believed that Charlotte was incredibly ordinary in so many ways – but that, at the same time, she was also one of the most astonishing and exceptional of women, someone brave enough to step outside her safe haven in Haworth and beyond the limited expectations of mid-19th-century women. Gordon was in a similar camp, believing that, when it comes to writing lives, there is no final truth.[17] But Gordon aimed to project the strength of Charlotte, rather than her suffering. Instead of seeing her as a victim, Gordon's Charlotte was a lot more fearless than previous biographers had given her credit for.

In the same year as Gordon's book came out, Juliet Barker's epic doorstopper, *The Brontës*, was published. Both books approached Charlotte in two very different ways: Gordon read her subject through her writing; and Barker did so through the life. In terms of mere information, the latter is quite frankly a lifesaver, acting as the unofficial encyclopaedia of Brontë students and scholars everywhere. This book, as well as my own PhD research, owes a great debt to her thorough scholarship and dedication.

Discovered in a private collection, this was claimed to be the only photo of the three sisters together. But experts have identified inconsistences in the women's clothing and facial features.

For Barker, previous biographers had not done the Brontë family justice. So, she set out to write a collective biography of all the family members in order to overthrow some of the embedded stereotypes that surrounded each of them. Instead of trying to challenge the homogeneous label 'the Brontës', Barker embraced the term. In her capable and meticulous hands, 'the Brontës' then became a conglomerate, a tightly knit group made up of distinct individuals. They cannot and should not, Barker argued, be separated. They were, in their way, an anomaly in life and literature.

The Brontës was also new in its exploration of newspaper archives and local records. By starting with the cold, hard facts, Barker was able to build up a full picture of the family's everyday lives, and the world within and beyond their front door. She wanted Anne, Emily, Charlotte, Branwell and Patrick's true identities and experiences to emerge from beneath the rubble of previous biographies. Her *raison d'être* was effectively to brush away, like thick, centuries-old cobwebs, the many fables and fictions still attached to the Brontë 'brand'.

A few years later, Lucasta Miller addressed these myths from a different angle. *The Brontë Myth* was a meta-biography that tracked the ever-changing approaches to the Brontës over the years, from moralistic Victorian anthologies to paraphernalia emblazoned with the sisters' faces. It also sought to unpick some of the inherent challenges faced by a biographer – the inevitability of imposing certain biases onto the family, and the question of what to leave in and what to take out. As Miller noted, this process often says more about the author and their generation than the Brontës themselves. If anything, she discovered the near impossibility of fully stripping away the myth surrounding the family. The stories about them, whether true or false, are so embedded in the cultural psyche that they are hard to disentangle and distinguish from 'reality'. We will perhaps never truly uncover the 'real' Charlotte.

Miller concluded the book with the expressed wish that we should, finally, be putting the family's writings first in our discussions. This could be the key to unveiling, if not a truer image of Charlotte and her siblings, then at least an alternative one. That was in 2001. Evidently, the task of shifting perceptions of a well-known writer takes time. Even in the supposedly enlightened 21st century, conversations about Charlotte centre on her sex life (or lack thereof) and her looks. We are still unable, or maybe just unwilling, to reframe our discussions of Charlotte and view her as a serious writer. She may be cited as one of the nation's best loved novelists and someone who changed the face of English literature, but she is still reduced to her gender.

One of the most tedious and persistent questions hovering over her head is that of her appearance: was she ugly? If this question was accompanied by an in-depth analysis of the changing cultural ideals of beauty and the ways in which such standards affect how we see ourselves in society, then it might make for interesting and illuminating reading. Yet, consistently and exhaustingly, critics and reviewers continue to obsess over Charlotte's appearance without any deeper exploration. It is simply the surface of her life, one at which we are encouraged to laugh or smirk. It reduces Charlotte to her sexuality. And it is ultimately the punchline of a cheap joke, devised to intrigue the reader's baser interests. Why else open your review of a new Brontë biography with this zinger: 'It can't be denied: Charlotte Brontë was no beauty'?[18] Similarly, another review had the headline 'Charlotte Brontë: Cinderella or Ugly Sister?' – despite the fact that the article itself made no real mention of Charlotte's apparent unattractiveness.[19]

The buzz surrounding Charlotte's lacklustre physicality stemmed from Claire Harman's 2015 biography, *Charlotte Brontë: A Life*. In it, Harman did discuss the various possible portraits of Charlotte, including a potential self-portrait – in effect, a 19th-century selfie. The image in question is, as

A Victorian model of demure female beauty.

Harman noted, not particularly flattering.[20] The woman's eyebrows are thick, dark and low, the forehead wide and high, the chin small, the eyes far apart. Charlotte was notoriously sensitive when it came to her looks, so it's unsurprising that she didn't depict herself as a beauty. Even if this is Charlotte herself, I'm not sure exactly what the image is meant to tell us. That, like most twenty-somethings, she wasn't entirely happy with her appearance? It is fascinating to understand how Charlotte saw herself, and how she thought others saw her – but Harman certainly did not fixate on whether or not Brontë was a beauty. That mania was, perhaps unsurprisingly, sparked by the media.

Notably, and unlike her fellow biographers, Harman's book came with no apology, no justification and no preface. She provided neither an agenda nor an aim. Instead, the biography opened with a moment of crisis, when, alone in Brussels, Charlotte wandered into a Catholic church and confessed – as a Protestant with strong anti-Catholic opinions, such a step was remarkable. Harman positioned this episode as a tipping point in Charlotte's life. At the time, she was in extremis, but this confessional release seems – in Harman's interpretation – to have clarified her ambition to write her own truth.[21] By the end of that year, she had already begun her first novel, *The Professor*. It was a kind of artistic liberation. In one sense, this analysis of Charlotte's crisis sustains the troublesome idea that much of her writing was itself confessional. The reader becomes the priest, while the author pours forth her secrets. But it also brings together Charlotte's two identities: her personal desperation catalysed her literary determination.

In one of the few screen adaptations of the Brontës' lives, Sally Wainwright's recent BBC biopic, *To Walk Invisible* (2016), gives us a living, breathing Charlotte. The one-off telefilm charts the three years leading up to the publication of *Jane Eyre, Wuthering Heights*, and *Agnes Grey* in 1847, which coincided with the deterioration and eventual death of Branwell. The biopic is visually remarkable. The parsonage as it would have been in the 1840s is brought to life in vivid detail. Wainwright has spoken of her intention to make it 'feel as authentic' as possible: 'It's not a chocolate box world.'[22] *To Walk Invisible* becomes, then, a visual attempt to dampen the 'Brontë myth' once more. There's violence, swearing, sex and alcoholism. This isn't simply to modernise their biography, to make it 'sexier'; it's because they didn't live in an idyllic sanctuary. They had to deal with the distressing, often chaotic reality of everyday life just like everyone else. In the lead-up to their literary success, they were dealing with the fallout of their brother's addiction, an episode in the family's history rarely considered in much depth. If we thought the Brontës were remarkable before, it is even more extraordinary to see these three women write their masterpieces on the living room table amidst such familial anguish.

Charlotte – played by Finn Atkins – is short and plain, with her hair scraped back tightly and a pair of small round glasses to squint through. Atkins plays the barely suppressed fieriness of Charlotte brilliantly. This Charlotte is slightly haughty and a bit bossy, as she convinces Anne (played by Charlie Murphy) and Emily (played by Chloe Pirrie) to publish their poetry pseudonymously. She is also shown as less sympathetic to Branwell's plight, but it's suggested that this stems from a source of envy. He has the freedom to do whatever he pleases, to be 'at it' with his employer's wife. Meanwhile, Charlotte can only dream of doing such a thing with Héger. Unlike her brother, she is subject to restrictions, which she seeks to override. It is a sympathetic portrayal, though, one that embraces her complexities rather than harmonising them. Her ambition and that defiant streak which comes through in her letters and novels, as well as the portraits of her, is all there. It's an affecting representation of a woman trying to pursue her dreams and keep it together while things fall apart around her.

Siv Jansson, the literary adviser for *To Walk Invisible*, writes that every biography 'presents a version of the family which responds to and represents its cultural moment'.[23] *To Walk Invisible* suggests we are ready to embrace another side of the Brontës' story, one reflective of our own cultural and social concerns. We don't want the 'chocolate box' image; we want something much darker. That's why there is so much violence in the biopic, as well as the inclusion of Yorkshire accents. Not only is it more realistic (regardless of what the detractors say, the Brontës would have spoken with Yorkshire burrs in some form), it also brings the Brontës closer to us as viewers and readers. As Rebecca Fraser maintained, Charlotte was both ordinary and extraordinary. *To Walk Invisible* captures this middle ground perfectly, with its mix of everyday tragedy and remarkable genius.

Claire Harman's book and Wainwright's biopic, then, feel like a watershed moments in Brontë biography. No longer do we have to compete with the hauntings of biographers past; the romantic myths have been dispelled and, in many ways, replaced with grittier ones. Can it be that, finally, something closer to the 'real Charlotte' can now emerge? It's a noble quest – but it seems unlikely.

After all, each of us has our own Charlotte Brontë.

THE MANY FACES OF CHARLOTTE BRONTË

There has been a longstanding fascination with Charlotte Brontë's appearance. As the possible self-portrait discussed in Harman's biography shows, we are still searching for a glimpse of Charlotte as she truly was.

This is partly because we don't really know what Charlotte looked like. Many of the unofficial (and even the official) paintings and images of Charlotte are contested or contentious. There are also no known photographs of her or her sisters. The photo at the beginning of this chapter was initially believed to be of Charlotte, taken within a year of her death in 1855 – but it is in fact of Ellen Nussey. Despite irrefutable confirmation of the sitter's identity, it remains an image strongly associated with the *Jane Eyre* author.

Another photograph, this time of three women, was discovered in a private collection in Scotland several years ago. The women are dressed in thick, dark capes, with one wearing an elaborate feathered hat and another staring fixedly ahead. The words '*Les Soeurs Brontë*' are written on the photo's reverse, a clue that the image can be traced to France. Robert Haley, who found the photo, believes the image cannot be 'anyone but' the Brontës.[24] While Haley has conducted his own research into the photograph, documented on his blog 'The Brontë Sisters

– A True Likeness?', experts have dated the image to the 1850s, after Anne and Emily's deaths, placing doubt on the photo's legitimacy. In 2015, another photo of three women purchased by Seamus Molloy on eBay was mooted as a potential rendering of the Brontës. This image was, again, dismissed by several researchers and considered with dubiety by the Brontë Parsonage Museum and Library.

Ann Dinsdale, Principal Curator at the Brontë Parsonage, poses the question: 'The thing you have to bear in mind is why would anyone have wanted to paint or photograph them at that time?'[25] They weren't famous until the late 1840s and, even then, their true identities were concealed for a time. It was also very unusual, not to say expensive, to have a photograph taken in the 1840s. In Charlotte's many letters, there is no mention of visiting a photographer.

Despite this healthy dose of scepticism, the possible portraits and photographs keep on coming. In 2017, a painting allegedly of the three Brontës by Edwin Landseer, dated 1834, was sold for £50,000. Yet many experts remain unconvinced of its authenticity. James Gorin von Grozny, an art collector who bought the painting in 2009, believes Landseer met the Brontë sisters at Bolton Abbey during their daytrip there in 1833. Landseer's 1834 painting, 'Bolton Abbey in the Olden Times', matches up in terms of dates. And his friend, John Nussey, was the brother of Ellen, so there is a family connection, however tenuous. But, as with the photographs, the question remains: why would Landseer paint three unknown young women? They weren't 'the Bells' at that time. There is no concrete evidence that Landseer met Charlotte and her sisters; and, again, there is no mention of the episode in their letters. In the absence of undeniable proof, a narrative has been created around the image. We discover a painting and something about it resonates. That moment of recognition takes on a life of its own, blurring the edges between fact and fiction in an attempt to bring us closer to Charlotte, Anne and Emily Brontë.

The instinct to create stories from portraits of Charlotte is reflected in this book's cover. It's a colourised version of Alonzo Chappel's 1870s engraving, itself a reworking of George Richmond's officially (and the only) commissioned portrait of Charlotte Brontë from 1850, now owned by the National Portrait Gallery. While Chappel's image is not 'official', in that it was not taken from life, it is symbolic of the repeated re-imaginings of her face and the attempts to bring the woman and the writer together in one frame, making it a fitting choice for a book on 21st-century perceptions of Charlotte.

In Chappel's image, the face, hair and necktie are taken from Richmond's sketch, but Charlotte has been prettified, her features softened and made more proportional. While her gaze remains steady and enigmatic, as in Richmond's portrait, there is now the hint of a demure Mona Lisa smile. The book in her hand is closed and she is looking into the distance, as if listening placidly to someone who has just interrupted her reading. It is, from this reading, a safe image. But part of me also reads – or wants to read – an element of defiance in her gaze.

The paradoxical readings of Charlotte Brontë are embodied in Chappel's image and illustrated nicely by Amber K. Regis and Deborah Wynne. They note Chappel's attempts to bring together the two seemingly oppositional sides of Charlotte Brontë: 'woman and writer'. She is given a 'glamorous, sexualised' figure 'with a narrow waist and full skirts,' but the 'implied presence of a corset also suggests strict regulation, her body conforming to nineteenth-century moral and medical strictures'.[26] The book in her hand is also a contradictory symbol. Of course, it represents her writerly status. Yet it is also 'held casually, carelessly, tilted away from her gaze' as if in complete disregard of its meaning.[27] Regis and Wynne conclude that, while her authorship is 'explicitly invoked' in Chappel's etching, it is ultimately 'overwritten by multiple signifiers of idealised femininity'.[28] Even when Charlotte's literary prowess is evoked, femininity is always imposed on her.

When examining Richmond's professional portrait of Charlotte, as it hung above the fireplace in the parsonage, Patrick Brontë fancied he could 'see strong indications, of the Genius, of the Author, of "Shirley", and "Jane Eyre"'.[29] It is perhaps this indication of genius which I read into Chappel's image, too. When I think of what Charlotte Brontë looked like, that enigmatic, impenetrable gaze comes to mind, reflecting the boldness of her writing and its ability to be revisited repeatedly, always with something new to notice. Yet Patrick's words also suggest that the signs of genius were less readily identifiable in Charlotte's everyday countenance than in the etching. Of course, this makes sense, as Patrick knew Charlotte first and foremost as his daughter, not as the author of *Shirley* and *Jane Eyre*. But it does disclose a division between how we see a person in life and what we see in their portrait.

As Regis and Wynne write: 'more than ever, we are driven to imagine Charlotte's face anew, hoping to recognise within the lines of a portrait or photograph the very person, or personality, that we feel we know'.[30] For Alice Spawls, we Brontëites 'seem to want images too much, and not find it odd that there are so many incompatible ones floating about, all said to be likenesses

Illustration by John H. Bacon, c. 1897.

of a person for whom we have no reliable portrait'.[31] The persistent need to assign more and more portraits to the Brontës suggests, however, a deep uneasiness with all of the images, reliable or otherwise. None of them seems to capture entirely our notions of Charlotte Brontë. Perhaps what is truly odd is our inability to accept that the competing likenesses are all representative of Charlotte in one form or another.

Without a photograph at hand, or any definitive 'evidence' of what Charlotte looked like, we have been trying to fill in the blanks. It is another attempt to fix her image, to say without doubt: *this* is Charlotte Brontë. In the end, what these images and portrayals reiterate is that there are multiple versions of Charlotte, as an author and as a woman. As Spawls queries, with scepticism: 'Does it matter if it isn't really a portrait of them, or doesn't look like them, so long as we know what it stands for?'[32] Why do we want to fix her image? The process of discovering the 'real' Charlotte is infinite; it will only end when the interest in her life and work recedes, if at all. The writer who wished to be 'for ever known', but also revelled in the ability 'to walk invisible', lies somewhere in-between.[33] These contradictions are fundamental to our understanding of Charlotte Brontë. She is recognisable, almost instantly; and yet her image resists incontrovertible fixity. She remains, physically at least, unrecoverable – and that is surely part of the appeal.

BEYOND THE BIOGRAPHICAL

In the 21st century, there have been several artistic reimaginings of Charlotte's *Jane Eyre*. These artworks and adaptations distil the novel to its very essence – whatever that may be – and, from that, convert the book's power into a different medium. It is a transformative process, one that often challenges and contradicts our safe assumptions of Charlotte and her work.

The next couple of passages give an overview of two modern re-workings of *Jane Eyre*, in art and in theatre. Their approaches differ: the former is fixed on canvas and yet changes whenever viewed by new eyes; the latter has a kinetic energy, capturing the movement of the novel and the restlessness of its heroine. But both crystallise their own reading of *Jane Eyre*, as well as its ongoing impact on the national, and global, imagination. Readers and viewers still respond on an emotional, but also physical level to the story, recognising parts of themselves in its pages, still shocked by the heat of its passages.

Like Charlotte's biographies, what these current re-tellings prove is the constant need to re-evaluate our connection with her work, and that Charlotte's classic tale still speaks directly to us.

Paula Rego's Jane Eyre

Rego's twenty-five *Jane Eyre* lithographs (2001–2) bring to life the novel's dark and disturbing side. They distort scale and size, and refuse to prettify the characters, even the statuesque St John Rivers. This was just as Charlotte intended – her purpose was to create a heroine as poor, plain and obscure as herself.[34] Unlike her sisters, she felt it was 'morally wrong' to make characters beautiful, and that her plain Jane would be just as interesting regardless of appearance.[35] In this sense, Charlotte's awareness of beauty standards fed directly into her writing.

The fact that Rego adhered to Charlotte's original resolution was, in itself, ground-breaking. Previous representations of Jane Eyre had been flawless and angelic, like Joan Fontaine, or unconventionally but ethereally beautiful. Rego didn't play along. In her characteristic style, she accentuated features, twisting people's faces and forms out of shape. There is an uncanniness to all of the lithographs, something deeply disconcerting. The drawings are both realistic and exaggerated, so that they become instantly recognisable and yet somehow alien.

Most of the illustrations – or anti-illustrations, as they have been called – portray Jane as an adult, even when the image depicts a scene from her childhood.[36] This was perhaps intended to reflect Rego's own discovery of the novel in later life.[37] But it's also an acknowledgement of Jane's own adulthood. As a narrator, she is looking back on her life from the vantage point of a mother and a wife, at least ten years on from 'Reader, I married him'. The romantic, and indeed erotic, potential of her story was not lost on Jane. Rego also recognised it, and all of her etchings are infused with a sensuality that can be unsettling at times.

Take, for example, 'Loving Bewick', one of the best known in the collection. It sees Jane sitting with her head tilted back, eyes closed. A pelican sits on her lap and the tip of its beak touches Jane's open mouth. This is an ode to Jane's consuming fascination with Thomas Bewick's *History of British Birds* (see Chapter Three), a book that let her escape the everyday violence and neglect at Gateshead with her aunt and cousins. But, in Rego's version, it's unclear as to whether Jane is being fed or assaulted by the bird. Marina Warner has described this as Eucharistic, a form of rapture, thereby seeing it as a kind of spiritual nourishment.[38] Cora Kaplan, however, noted the violent undertones of the drawing, its hint at submission and violation.[39] In light of the novel's representation of Bewick, it's likely that Warner's interpretation is closest.

But Rego's lithographs were never meant to be directly linked to Charlotte's novel. Inspired by it, perhaps, but not imitations of it. They are stand-alone pieces that not only inform how we see Jane, but also how we see Rego and even ourselves. If anything, her *Jane Eyre* collection is a testament to the novel's uncontainable impact on culture. The issues it deals with have almost outgrown the book's pages, spilling over into our everyday cultural language as a shared understanding, no longer dependent on the work itself.

21st-Century Jane

The theatre production of *Jane Eyre*, staged at Bristol and London from 2014 to 2016, has been one of the most original modern re-imaginings of the classic in recent times. In 2013, Sally Cookson began work on her radical reworking of the novel. Split over two performances for its Bristol audience, then condensed into one for its London run, the play adapted Charlotte's novel for a 21st-century audience while maintaining its core message: that all humans deserve love and liberty. By taking one of the most recognisable books in English literature, stripping it back and re-imagining the essence of the story for the stage, Cookson and her team created a testament to the durability of Charlotte's work.

Unlike Virginia Woolf, Sally Cookson wanted to prove that *Jane Eyre* was a life story, not just a love story. Curiously, almost 170 years after its publication, such an approach to the novel is refreshing. Yet, when you consider the continued pigeonholing of female authors into the neat sub-genre entitled 'women writers', perhaps it is not so curious. Why do we so often still reduce

Charlotte – and the entire Brontë family – remain as popular as ever, and the museum in Haworth attracts countless visitors.

Jane Eyre – and *Wuthering Heights*, for that matter – to simple, simpering romances? Don't get me wrong: I love a good period drama complete with a bit of swooning and the obligatory Colin-Firth-in-a-wet-shirt scene (or its baby-oiled equivalent – thanks, Poldark). But, when some of the most ingenious and ground-breaking novels in the English canon are remembered as love stories first and foremost, you can be forgiven for wondering why.

What Sally Cookson's production showed more than anything was that Charlotte remains as relevant as ever. In several interviews and articles following the success of the play's initial run at the Bristol Old Vic, Cookson spoke of *Jane Eyre*'s preoccupation with the necessity of basic human rights: the fact that all individuals need to be fed not only physically, but also emotionally, spiritually and intellectually (much like Rego's 'Loving Bewick' suggests).[40] In order to capture this need, the play follows Jane from her own birth to the birth of her child with Rochester. In a triumphant twist, the ending echoes the production's opening with the cry of a baby – first, Jane and, finally, her child – and the announcement, 'It's a girl' (in the novel, Jane and Rochester have a boy). The finale makes you want to punch the air, but a standing ovation sufficed. Despite starting out as an unloved and uncared for orphan – notably Cookson's play doesn't see Jane inherit a fortune from her uncle – Jane's indomitable spirit prevails, and her daughter's noisy entrance into the world heralds hope for the future. The symmetry of the play is also tinged with a bittersweet acknowledgement of the cycle of human suffering and survival. Like her, Jane's daughter may find herself without her loved ones, and forced to fall back on nothing but her own resolve.

The stage, as one reviewer noted, looked like an adventure-play-ground, with its monkey bars to swing on and platforms to jump from.[41] This aided the introduction of the fluid, balletic move-ments that signalled the various shifts in time, place and emotion, as the play whizzed through Jane's formative years in the space of three and a half hours. The addition of windows – through which Jane was often looking or trying to break – evoked the competing forces of freedom and entrapment at work in the narrative. And, then, there was the music. Benji Bower created the soundtrack of this *Jane Eyre*, made up of folkloric songs, pop tunes and eerie melodies. The music often stands in

Motherhood, Jane's destiny, was not to be for Charlotte herself.

for Jane's inner thoughts, giving the audience an insight into her complex world within. Yet it is the deep, reverberating voice of Melanie Marshall, who plays the ever-lurking yet always silent (in terms of speech) Bertha Mason, that still sings in the memory days later.

The decision to have Bertha onstage throughout the play, instead of revealing her dramatically halfway through, highlights the connection between herself and Jane. Both women are trapped in society's narrow standards; both women have fallen for the 'charms' of Mr Rochester. As we see Jane slowly recognise her love for Rochester, Bertha appears in a red dress to sing Noel Coward's 'Mad About the Boy'. Its lyrics – suggesting that the love interest is something of a 'cad' – apply to both Bertha and Jane's situations. Bertha has been discarded as a wife and left to deteriorate in the attic, while Rochester rides around Europe to escape his guilt; and Jane knows of Rochester's past transgressions, his old caddish ways. Both, in their own way, are mad about him.

Similarly, when Jane flees Thornfield, having discovered that Rochester is already married, Bertha reappears onstage. This time, she sings a slower version of Gnarls Barkley's 'Crazy' and its effect is electric – not only is Bertha 'mad', as Rochester claims, but Jane's own mental stability is questioned in this moment of estrangement and dislocation. Although the notion of Bertha symbolising the passionate side of Jane is nothing new (in their seminal literary criticism, *The Madwoman in the Attic*, Sandra Gilbert and Susan Gubar described Bertha as Jane's 'avatar'), seeing the two women onstage together, their narratives entwined through music, felt like a radical reinterpretation of their relationship.[42]

The script, music and movement were devised during rehearsal, with the cast, director, designers and musicians all informing the onstage unfolding of the story. This collective creativity meant each member of the team was fully invested in the progression of Jane's life story. Their collaborative production responded to the novel's enduring subversive nature, the fact that it remains modern and revolutionary in so many ways. As with so many admirers of Charlotte, myself included, Cookson envisaged her creative power as a fire. She referred to the book as 'incendiary', a spark waiting to be lit under society's conventions.[43] In writing her book, then, Charlotte became an imaginary arsonist, and Jane Eyre was the catalyst.

The flames of her work continue to burn to this day.

THREE

CHARLOTTE
IN NATURE

A view of the northern landscape by Thomas Bewick.

Think of the Brontës and I'd wager you almost instinctively see the Yorkshire moors in your mind's eye. The two are so closely aligned in most people's imagination that it can be difficult to think of Charlotte in any other place. After all, large sections of her books – particularly *Jane Eyre* and *Shirley* – are set firmly in that same dramatic, windswept landscape. On top of that, she is certainly not shy of using 'pathetic fallacies' in her work (attributing human emotions to nature). So, when the tree at Thornfield gets hit by lightning on the night of Jane and Rochester's engagement, you know something's afoot.

But it would be too simplistic to dismiss Charlotte's scene-painting as mere descriptions of the nature on her own door-step. Her fictional landscapes are not mirror images of the Haworth moors. Her ability to render her characters' sur-roundings so vividly comes from years of reading about, drawing and being in nature. From her love of the natural history author Thomas Bewick and Romantic poet William Wordsworth to her dedication to art, Charlotte's creativity was founded on seeing and expressing the natural world. Her nature writing is the culmination of these activities and passions, and it positions her as one of the original nature writers, a genre that has regained significance in recent years. Take this beautiful description of a winter's morning from *Shirley*, for example:

> It was now the middle of the month of February; by six o'clock, therefore, dawn was just beginning to steal on night, to penetrate with a pale ray its brown obscurity, and give a demi-translucence to its opaque shadows. Pale enough that ray was on this particular morning; no colour tinged the east, no flush warmed it. To see what a heavy lid day slowly lifted, what a wan glance she flung along the hills, you would have thought the sun's fire quenched in last night's floods. The breath of this morning was chill as its aspect; a raw wind stirred the mass of night-cloud, and showed, as it slowly rose – leaving a colourless, silver-gleaming ring all round the horizon – not blue sky, but a stratum of paler vapour beyond.[1]

Many of Charlotte's readers have admired her particular ability to portray nature in imaginative ways, but few will have considered that this aspect of her work is bang on trend today, given the explosion of nature writing's popularity over the last few years – just think of the huge success of books such as *H is for Hawk* by Helen Macdonald, or *The Shepherd's Life* by James Rebanks, to name just two recent examples.

In this chapter, I'm going to look at Charlotte's work in light of this resurgence in nature writing, to place her as a nature writer for our times and to show why authors – both in the 19th and 21st centuries – revert to nature as a means of understanding and coming closer to the world we inhabit.

A TALE OF TWO HAWORTHS

There is a gap between the Haworth that Charlotte knew and loved, and the one that readers and tourists see today. The Brontë Parsonage Museum does a great job in bridging this gap, by providing visitors with information on 19th-century Haworth's sanitary condition and how the lack of a sewage system damaged the townsfolk's health. This gives us a glimpse into how the people of Haworth, including the Brontë family, lived – and it isn't always pretty.

After Patrick Brontë and others mounted numerous petitions and protestations against the insanitary state of Haworth, Benjamin Babbage was finally sent from the General Board of Health in 1850 to inspect the sanitation and water supply of the village. He found a dire situation: 41.6% of the population died before their sixth birthday.[2] Between 1838 and 1849, the average age at death was 25.8. And the annual mortality rate per thousand was 25.4, making it 10.5% higher than the legal healthy level decreed by the government before serious intervention. It's fair to say that 21st-century Britain has come a long way since then.

Despite the predominant belief that the Brontës were isolated from society and culture, they were in fact very much aware of the Industrial Revolution and scientific progress. Haworth was a town of two halves: up the hill, behind the parsonage, you had (and still have) the rural 'wuthering' moors, the main image of the family that remains fixed in the popular imagination; down the hill, however, there were already thirteen textile mills in the vicinity of Haworth's chapelry when Patrick and Maria moved there.[3] The town was close to industrial hubs such as Keighley and Bradford, and was positioned on the road between Yorkshire and Lancashire – far from being a cultural and social backwater, Haworth was at the centre of industrial activity and, as the parson's daughter, Charlotte would have been in the midst of it.

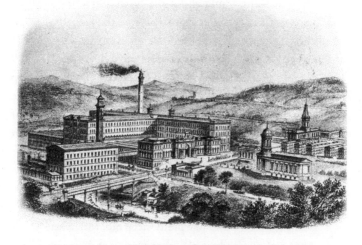

Yorkshire textile mills.

In contrast, the apparent rurality of the place is emphasised today by the fact that tourism has largely replaced the
heavy industries, and the streets below the parsonage are now
adorned with cafés with names such as 'Villette', shops selling
Brontë memorabilia, and busloads of visitors. But Haworth is
not just a Brontë haven. It has its own historical, quaint character with its steep, cobbled main street and higgledy-piggledy
Yorkshire stone buildings that, to modern eyes at least, give it
the air of a traditional rural idyll worthy of any picture-post-
card depiction of Britain's countryside.

The opening of Elizabeth Gaskell's enduringly popular *The
Life of Charlotte Brontë* shaped the perception of Haworth as
its own separate social bubble and, to an extent, continues to
perpetuate this view.[4] The romanticism of that image – a house
on top of a hill with nothing but graves for company – remains
inviting and this pull is intensified by the collective genius of
the house's inhabitants.

Gaskell had nous and she knew how to hook her readers.

There is something filmic about the biography's first chapter, which chronicles a traveller's journey from the large, industrial communities of Leeds and then Keighley to the microcosm of Haworth parsonage's doorsteps. In her description, Gaskell fails to mention the mill houses and factories on the road up to the parsonage. Instead, in keeping with her own romantic view of Charlotte's home life, she focuses on the wildness of Haworth's natural surroundings and its bleak loneliness, which is twinned with Charlotte's own solitariness:

> Right before the traveller on this road rises Haworth vil-
> lage; he can see it for two miles before he arrives, for it
> is situated on the side of a pretty steep hill, with a back-
> ground of dun and purple moors, rising and sweeping
> away yet higher than the church, which is built at the
> very summit of the long narrow street. All round the
> horizon there is this same line of sinuous wave-like hills;

High Sunderland Hall, possibly the inspiration for Heathcliff's home on the 'wild, bleak moors' in Emily's Wuthering Heights.

the scoops into which they fall only revealing other hills beyond, of similar colour and shape, crowned with wild, bleak moors—grand, from the ideas of solitude and lone-liness which they suggest, or oppressive from the feeling which they give of being pent-up by some monotonous and illimitable barrier, according to the mood of mind in which the spectator may be.

For a short distance the road appears to turn away from Haworth, as it winds round the base of the shoulder of a hill; but then it crosses a bridge over the 'beck,' and the ascent through the village begins. The flag-stones with which it is paved are placed end-ways, in order to give a better hold to the horses' feet; and, even with this help, they seem to be in constant danger of slipping back-wards. The old stone houses are high compared to the width of the street, which makes an abrupt turn before reaching the more level ground at the head of the village, so that the steep aspect of the place, in one part, is almost like that of a wall. But this surmounted, the church lies a little off the main road on the left; a hundred yards, or so, and the driver relaxes his care, and the horse breathes more easily, as they pass into the quite little by-street that leads to Haworth Parsonage. The churchyard is on one side of this lane, the school-house and the sexton's dwell-ing (where the curates formerly lodged) on the other.

The parsonage stands at right angles to the road, fac-ing down upon the church; so that, in fact, parsonage, church, and belfried school-house, form three sides of an irregular oblong, of which the fourth is open to the fields and moors that lie beyond. The area of this oblong is filled up by a crowded churchyard, and a small garden or court in front of the clergyman's house. As the entrance to this from the road is at the side, the path goes round the corner into the little plot of ground. Underneath the windows is a narrow flower-border, carefully tended in days of yore, although only the most hardy plants could be made to grow there. Within the stone wall, which keeps out the surrounding churchyard, are bushes of elder and lilac; the rest of the ground is occupied by a square grass-plot and a gravel walk. The house is of grey stone, two stories high, heavily roofed with flags, in order to resist the winds that might strip off a lighter covering. It appears to have been built about a hundred years ago, and to consist of four rooms on each story; the two windows on the right (as the visitor stands with his back to the church, ready to enter in at the front door) belonging to Mr. Brontë's study, the two on the left to the family sitting-room. Everything about the place tells of the most dainty order, the most exquisite cleanliness. The door-steps are spotless; the small old-fashioned window-panes glitter like looking-glass. Inside and outside of that house cleanliness goes up into its essence, purity.[5]

As Babbage's report discovered, there was nothing particularly 'pure' or 'spotless' about Haworth, but within the first few pages of the biography, Gaskell distances the parsonage from the unsanitary nature of the village and landscape surrounding it. Despite its proximity to major industrial centres, and despite the village's own manufacturing enterprises, the parsonage seems to inhabit its own little ecosystem. However, Charlotte was clearly not cut off from the world, and this is evident even in some of her nature writing. She of course focuses predominantly on the beauty of the countryside, but there is also undoubtedly an awareness of the threat posed by the forces of change, as is made clear by the 'sting in the tail' in this description of an autumnal landscape in *The Professor*:

Haworth Parsonage and graveyard.

A fine October morning succeeded to the foggy evening that had witnessed my first introduction to
Crimsworth Hall. I was early up and walking in the
large park-like meadow surrounding the house. The
autumn sun, rising over the —shire hills, disclosed a
pleasant country; woods brown and mellow varied the
fields from which the harvest had been lately carried;
a river, gliding between the woods, caught on its surface the somewhat cold gleam of the October sun and
sky; at frequent intervals along the banks of the river,
tall cylindrical chimneys, almost slender round towers,
indicated the factories which the trees half concealed;
here and there mansions, similar to Crimsworth Hall,
o–ccupied agreeable sites on the hill side; the country wore, on the whole, a cheerful, active, fertile look.
Steam, trade, machinery had long banished from it all
romance and seclusion.[6]

A photograph of Haworth parsonage taken in the 1860s – not so long after Charlotte died in 1855 – perhaps tells us about the reality of living there during the mid-19th century. Today, the house is surrounded by tall trees planted in the graveyard after Babbage's report in 1850, blocking out any clear view of the surrounding moors. In this older picture of Haworth, however, there are no trees. The house looks oddly exposed and vulnerable. Charlotte's view from her window would have been very different to the view seen by visitors today. Even this shift in perspective makes us rethink Charlotte's outlook on nature. The house is now enclosed by greenery, chiming with Gaskell's account of the parsonage's remoteness. Instead of being shielded, however, Charlotte had full access to the landscape surrounding her home and to the village below. This openness meant she was in tune with the changing of seasons, the weather and the wildlife, all of which fed into her artful representation of nature.

THE ROMANTICS

The novels and poems Charlotte read in childhood also helped to mould her work. And, considering the Brontë siblings' love of the Romantic poets, it is little wonder that the natural world has such a central role in her writing. William Wordsworth and the Lake District poets greatly influenced the Brontë children, so much so that Branwell even wrote to the elderly Wordsworth, in the hope that the great poet would offer him some literary advice and even mentorship. Unfortunately, Wordsworth was less than impressed with Branwell's poetry or his claim that there was 'not a *writing* poet worth a sixpence', a comment to which Wordsworth perhaps (and understandably) took offence on behalf of some of his writing friends.[7] He never replied.

Around the same time, Charlotte wrote to another of the Lake Poets, the Poet Laureate Robert Southey. Unlike

Ashness Bridge and Derwentwater: inspiration for the Romantics.

Wordsworth to Branwell, Southey replied to Charlotte's letter – but in less than encouraging words (see also Chapter Five). Although he praised her writing, telling her that she possessed 'in no inconsiderable degree what Wordsworth call[ed] "the faculty of Verse"', he emphasised that literature 'cannot be the business of a woman's life'.[8] Thankfully, Charlotte ignored this last point.

The siblings' lack of success in their correspondences with Romantic poets did not curtail their admiration of them. If Charlotte's successors to nature writing are Richard Mabey and Sara Maitland, then her predecessors – the writers whom she read as a child and filled her imagination – have to be Wordsworth, Southey and, of course, Lord Byron. Byron had a profound influence on Charlotte's writing: from her youthful work, with all its Byronic heroes, to *Villette* and its Gothic undertones. Without Byron's brooding narrators, such as Don Juan, there might never have been the irascible and mysterious Mr Rochester. But Byron's articulation of nature in his epic *Childe Harold's Pilgrimage* (such as here in Canto III, LXXI–LXXII) may also have had an impact on the young Charlotte:

Is it not better, then, to be alone,
And love Earth only for its earthly sake?
By the blue rushing of the arrowy Rhone,
Or the pure bosom of its nursing lake,
Which feeds it as a mother who doth make
A fair but froward infant her own care,
Kissing its cries away as these awake;—
Is it not better thus our lives to wear,
Than join the crushing crowd, doomed to inflict or bear?

I live not in myself, but I become
Portion of that around me; and to me,
High mountains are a feeling, but the hum
Of human cities torture: I can see
Nothing to loathe in Nature, save to be
A link reluctant in a fleshly chain,
Classed among creatures, when the soul can flee,
And with the sky, the peak, the heaving plain
Of ocean, or the stars, mingle, and not in vain.[9]

If we're thinking of Charlotte and her family from the perspective of the Brontë myth, lines such as 'to me / High mountains are a feeling, but the hum / Of human cities torture' match the popular perception of her as a loner who preferred the company of nature to that of people. This opinion of Charlotte has quite rightly been tempered in recent years, but Byron's words would have rung true in the parsonage, especially after the deaths of Branwell, Emily and Anne. Charlotte did find London a vibrating, jostling, nerve-wrecking city. And the feeling she imbues into her environmental descriptions proves she felt an affinity with nature. It was part of her home; it filled and surrounded her life. It was, as Byron wrote, a 'portion' of her identity.

Nature was a companion to all of the Brontës: both while walking outside on the hills and when reading a book inside. And so much of being in nature involves being alone or silent. There is a natural solitariness involved in enjoying the outside world. This is in many ways an individualistic experience, one that can be simplified to a harmonious communion between an individual and the environment. Yet the connection described by Byron and Wordsworth, the emotional pull between a person and a high mountain, is also based on the erasure of the individual. Nature can often be viewed as a constant; a place visited years before remains the same even though the visitor has altered. It is self-sufficient, moving along without the need for human intervention. In this vastness, you can better understand the wider world and your part in it. Wordsworth's 'Lines Written a Few Miles above Tintern Abbey, 1798' evokes this clearly:

Byron.

> And this prayer I make,
> Knowing that Nature never did betray
> The heart that loved her; 'tis her privilege,
> Through all the years of this our life, to lead
> From joy to joy: for she can so inform
> The mind that is within us, so impress
> With quietness and beauty, and so feed
> With lofty thoughts, that neither evil tongues,
> Rash judgments, nor the sneers of selfish men,
> Nor greetings where no kindness is, nor all
> The dreary intercourse of daily life,
> Shall e'er prevail against us, or disturb
> Our cheerful faith that all which we behold

Is full of blessings. Therefore let the moon
Shine on thee in thy solitary walk;
And let the misty mountain winds be free
To blow against thee: and in after years,
When these wild ecstasies shall be matured
Into a sober pleasure, when thy mind
Shall be a mansion for all lovely forms,
Thy memory be as a dwelling-place
For all sweet sounds and harmonies; Oh! then,
If solitude, or fear, or pain, or grief,
Should be thy portion, with what healing thoughts
Of tender joy wilt thou remember me,
And these my exhortations![10]

Charlotte's depictions of the world around her are a testament to her own Romantic awareness of nature and her place in it. In *Shirley* she uses the comically coarse character of Reverend Malone in order to give a tongue-in-cheek alternative to what Wordsworth so beautifully described in 'Tintern Abbey'. While Malone tramps through fields simply in order to reach his destination, the narrator – who is not necessarily Charlotte herself – notes all the natural splendour that Malone fails to admire:

Grasmere and surrounding fells, Wordsworth's home.

The evening was pitch-dark: star and moon were quenched in grey rain-clouds – grey they would have been by day, by night they looked sable. Malone was not a man given to close observation of Nature; her changes passed, for the most part, unnoticed by him: he could walk miles on the most varying April day, and never see the beautiful dallying of earth and heaven; never mark when a sunbeam kissed the hill-tops, making them smile clear in green light, or when a shower wept over them, hiding their crests with the low-hanging, dishevelled tresses of a cloud. He did not, therefore, care to contrast the sky as it now appeared – a muffled, streaming vault, all black, save where, towards the east, the furnaces of Stilbro' ironworks threw a tremulous lurid shimmer on the horizon – with the same sky on an unclouded frosty night. He did not trouble himself to ask where the constellations and the planets were gone, or to regret the 'black-blue' serenity of the air-ocean which those white islets stud; and which another ocean, of heavier and denser element, now rolled below and concealed. He just doggedly pursued his way, leaning a little forward as he walked, and wearing his hat on the back of his head, as his Irish manner was.[11]

Irish jokes aside, this passage is vivid and painterly in the way it brings together the natural and industrial elements of the West Riding environment. The image of the sky as an 'air-ocean' with its own 'white islets' is a beautiful example of Charlotte's ability to imaginatively reconstruct nature with words. The passage is also funny. It doesn't matter whether Malone is Irish or English or anything – to someone with an appreciation for the environment, the idea that anyone could be oblivious to the spectacle above and around them is amusing. Like Wordsworth, Charlotte knew the power of nature and she was ready to poke fun at those less enlightened.

Bewick's 'Yellow owl, gillihowlet, church, barn, or screech owl'.

NATURE WRITING

Thomas Bewick's *A History of British Birds*, published in 1797 and reprinted in expanded form in 1804, was central to Charlotte's childhood and shaped her relationship with the natural world. The detailed minutiae of his drawn vignettes – including scenes of ships and fields, as well as birds such as the great auk – influenced the Brontë children's own artistic and literary endeavours. Between 1829 and 1830, Charlotte and Branwell made numerous tiny books (no bigger than 2.5 by 5 centimetres) filled with minuscule sketches, stories and poems.

During the same period, Charlotte copied several of Bewick's drawings to hone her own sketching skills. These delicate drawings capture the intricacy of Bewick's own work, although it must be said that they are less perfect, less textbook. Their smudged messiness only adds to their charm, though. Sadly, Charlotte had to give up on drawing, as her dedication

to copying 'nimini-pimini' – that's Yorkshire for 'very small' –
engravings weakened her eyesight.[12] Blame Bewick. In 1834,
however, Charlotte still held Bewick in high esteem, advising
her best friend Ellen to read him for a lesson in natural history.[13] And in 1847, Bewick's *A History of British Birds* featured
in *Jane Eyre* as Jane's means of imaginative escape from her
aunt's home:

> I returned to my book – Bewick's *History of British Birds*:
> the letterpress thereof I cared little for, generally speak-
> ing; and yet there were certain introductory pages that,
> child as I was, I could not pass quite as a blank. They were
> those which treat of the haunts of sea-fowl; of 'the soli-
> tary rocks and promontories' by them only inhabited; of
> the coast of Norway, studded with isles from its southern
> extremity, the Lindeness, or Naze, to the North Cape –
>
> > 'Where the Northern Ocean, in vast whirls,
> > Boils round the naked, melancholy isles
> > Of farthest Thule; and the Atlantic surge
> > Pours in among the stormy Hebrides.'
>
> Nor could I pass unnoticed the suggestion of the bleak
> shores of Lapland, Siberia, Spitzbergen, Nova Zembla,
> Iceland, Greenland, with 'the vast sweep of the Arctic
> Zone, and those forlorn regions of dreary space' ... Of
> these death-white realms I formed an idea of my own:
> shadowy, like all the half-comprehended notions that
> float dim through children's brains, but strangely impres-
> sive ... Each picture told a story; mysterious often to my
> undeveloped understanding and imperfect feelings, yet
> ever profoundly interesting [...] With Bewick on my
> knee, I was then happy: happy at least in my way.[14]

Jane sees her surroundings through several mediums and from various perspectives. She peers into Bewick's *A History of British Birds* as if it is a window into another world. Later, at Lowood School and during a sleepless night, she seeks the comfort of a literal window and its view of the blue-lit hills. As a governess, she climbs to the top of Thornfield Hall and looks out over the horizon, hoping for 'a power of vision which might overpass that limit'.[15] By the time she arrives at the green isolation of Ferndean and is reunited with Rochester, Jane has gained this power of vision. Unlike her husband-to-be, who is now blind, she has the ability to see the world around her. She remains connected to nature through sight and maintains the ability to define her identity through her vision of the world and her physical place in it.

Thankfully, like Jane, Charlotte kept her eyesight. Rather ironically, however, she used to close her eyes while writing. Since she could no longer draw as intently as she used to, she chose to paint vivid scenes of natural beauty with words. Her proximity to the moors meant that she was able to learn the nuances of each season, allowing her to visualise the images in her mind and reproduce them on the page. Charlotte had a personal sensitivity to nature that you can feel in her work, one that also helps you to see the forests and fields of her imagination.

Charlotte and today's wildlife writers, such as Kathleen Jamie and Jim Crumley, were drawn towards writing about nature by similar impulses. Charlotte grew up in Yorkshire during the Industrial Revolution, when society was changing rapidly and the natural world was under threat from factory smoke and city expansion. And the 21st century has so far experienced a global financial crisis and numerous ecological disasters, placing our natural heritage in peril. Both periods were and are defined by instability and the urgency to act; in response, their respective writers turn to nature.

Bewick's level of detail in such small illustrations is extraordinary.

The proximity of Haworth to industrial epicentres made it difficult for the Brontës not to notice the rapidity of change in the North. Branwell's ill-fated stint on the Leeds and Manchester Railway at Sowerby Bridge and Luddenden Foot was a sign of such progress, even if his family – particularly Charlotte – weren't too impressed by his position as a head railway clerk. Through the railway, technology and its accompanying billows of smoke became a fixed part of the British landscape and subsequently enabled people who could afford it to move more freely. When Anne and Charlotte rushed to London to reveal their female identities to the publishers Smith, Elder & Co, they took an overnight train, cutting their journey time considerably. During another trip to London following her literary success, Charlotte visited the Great Exhibition five times. At first she called it a 'mighty Vanity Fair' in reference to Thackeray's serialised *Vanity Fair*; and later, guided by Sir David Brewster (who invented the kaleidoscope) she found the array of objects and inventions overwhelming, to the point that the exhibition took on a supernatural quality. She wrote to her father on the subject on 7 June 1851:

> Yesterday I went for the second time to the Crystal Palace—
> we remained in it about three hours—and I must say I was
> more struck with it on this occasion tha[n] at my first visit.
> It is a wonderful place—vast—strange new and impossible
> to describe. Its grandeur does not consist in *one* thing but
> in the unique assemblage of *all* things—Whatever human
> industry has created—you find there—from the great com-
> partments filled with Railway Engines and boilers, with
> Mill-machinery in full work [...] to the glass-covered and
> velvet spread stands loaded with the most gorgeous work of
> the goldsmith and silversmith [...] It seems as if magic only
> could have gathered this mass of wealth from all the ends
> of the Earth—as if none but supernatural hands could have
> arranged it thus—with such a blaze and contrast of colours
> and marvellous power of effect.[16]

The machinery and creations were almost magical because
they were alienated from their original purpose. In an exhibition space, they no longer inhabited the normal world that
Charlotte was used to and understood. Back in Yorkshire, the
view from Haworth over Keighley's factory chimneys and thick
smog was a constant reminder of the utilitarian industriousness
that was fast making its mark on Britain's landscape.

These changes acted as a foil to the expansive, bleak beauty
of the valley in which these towns and villages resided. Both
nature and capitalist industry can be dark and inhospitable at
times, and pollutants emitted from chimneys can merge with fog
to form toxic smogs. But Charlotte and her siblings always had
the moors as respite from the relentlessness of scientific progress. The natural world, particularly the weather and the changing seasons, were of significance even in the everyday lives of
the Brontës. In *The Life of Charlotte Brontë* Elizabeth Gaskell
describes Charlotte's propensity for noting changes in the sky:

I was struck by Miss Brontë's careful examination of the
shape of the clouds and the signs of the heavens, in which
she read, as from a book, what the coming weather would
be. I told her that I saw she must have a view equal in
extent at her own home. She said I was right, but that the
character of the prospect from Haworth was very different; that I had no idea what a companion the sky became
to any one living in solitude, – more than any inanimate
object on earth, – more than the moors themselves.[17]

Typically, Gaskell returns to Charlotte's isolation –
although, it's also true that Charlotte herself told Gaskell of
her own loneliness in this respect. Regardless of whatever
agenda Gaskell was trying to promote here, Charlotte's reliance on the sky as a friend, a source of knowledge and an
inspiration is indisputable. Such acuity shaped Charlotte's
own nature writing, so much so that it wouldn't look out of
place next to the likes of Robert MacFarlane, perhaps today's
foremost nature writer.

Crystal Palace, 1851: 'A wonderful place—vast'.

Changing Seasons

As Gaskell perceptively noted, for Charlotte, the sky was one vast, changeable book to be read on a daily basis. Her sensitivity to the sky's temperamental shifts emerges in her writing, where she translates the movements and colours of the 'air-ocean' into words. The changing of seasons was no different.

Jane Eyre in particular charts the seasons alongside its tracing of Jane's life. Traditionally, the changing seasons are a metaphor for the different stages of life. It makes sense, then, for Jane's 'autobiography' (the novel's subtitle) to reference spring, summer, autumn and winter. The novel begins with Jane's spring, her childhood, leading through its romantic but temperamental summer with Rochester, and slowly into its more stable, mellow autumn period – all from the perspective of a much older Jane, looking back from the winter of her life:

> Spring drew on: she was indeed already come; the frosts of winter had ceased; its snows were melted, its cutting winds ameliorated. My wretched feet, flayed and swollen to lameness by the sharp air of January, began to heal and subside under the gentler breathings of April; the nights and mornings no longer by their Canadian temperature froze the very blood in our veins; we could now endure the play-hour passed in the garden: sometimes on a sunny day it began even to be pleasant and genial, and a greenness grew over those brown beds, which, freshening daily, suggested the thought that Hope traversed them at night, and left each morning brighter traces of her steps. Flowers peeped out amongst the leaves; snow-drops, crocuses, purple auriculas, and golden-eyed pansies. On Thursday afternoons (half-holidays) we now took walks, and found still sweeter flowers opening by the wayside, under the hedges [...]

The heron: often spotted in Brontë country (Bewick).

April advanced to May: a bright serene May it was; days of blue sky, placid sunshine, and soft western or southern gales filled up its duration. And now vegetation matured with vigour; Lowood shook loose its tresses; it became all green, all flowery; its great elm, ash, and oak skeletons were restored to majestic life; woodland plants sprang up profusely in its recesses; unnumbered varieties of moss filled its hollows, and it made a strange ground-sunshine out of the wealth of its wild primrose plants: I have seen their pale gold gleam in overshadowed spots like scatterings of the sweetest lustre. All this I enjoyed often and fully, free, unwatched, and almost alone [...][18]

The seasons are vividly recalled by Jane. As she remembers her time at Lowood School, she relives the weather and subliminally connects the presence of trees, flowers and sunshine with her uplifted, more optimistic outlook. One particularly striking passage appears in *Jane Eyre*, in which Charlotte's study of the sky and seasons pays off:

I discovered, too, that a great pleasure, an enjoyment which the horizon only bounded, lay all outside the high and spike-guarded walls of our garden: this pleasure consisted in prospect of noble summits girdling a great hill-hollow, rich in verdure and shadow; in a bright beck, full of dark stones and sparkling eddies. How different had this scene looked when I viewed it laid out beneath the iron sky of winter, stiffened in frost, shrouded with snow!—when mists as chill as death wandered to the impulse of east winds along those purple peaks, and rolled down 'ing' and holm till they blended with the frozen fog of the beck! That beck itself was then a torrent, turbid and curbless: it tore asunder the wood, and sent a raving sound through the air, often thickened with wild rain or whirling sleet; and for the forest on its banks, *that* showed only ranks of skeletons.[19]

Nature and its horizon becomes a symbol of freedom, something that Jane is constantly seeking. It affects her mood – what we would now call seasonable affective disorder (SAD) – so that the volatility of nature informs her emotions and decisions, how she sees her place in the world. The description here is not simply a metaphor for Jane's inner mind, though; it's also showing nature and its nuances for its own sake. We don't just read nature through Jane's eyes or as a medium through which we understand Jane's psyche. For Charlotte, nature was not merely a memory or a force that she noticed occasionally. It was a major presence in her life and, by extension, a major character in her writing.

FOUR

MAGICAL
CHARLOTTE

'Eliciting from the gloom some haloed face...' (from Jane Eyre).

Charlotte is often seen as a writer of realism. She famously had a pop at the unrealistically romanticised neatness of Jane Austen's novels, likening them to 'a carefully-fenced, highly cultivated garden with neat borders and delicate flowers'.[1] And that's not even the worst bit (I think it's fair to say that Charlotte misunderstood Austen by taking her at face value and therefore failing to see her intrinsic irony). Charlotte preferred a rougher approach that reflected the reality of people's actual lives. But her work as an adult, like *Jane Eyre* and *Shirley*, is also heavily influenced by her early dalliance with the supernatural.

During her childhood and teenage years, Charlotte honed her narrative technique by creating the imaginary worlds of the Glass Town Federation and the kingdom of Angria. Alongside Branwell (and initially with Emily and Anne before they formed their own offshoot realm of Gondal), Charlotte wrote about a fictional African empire founded on civil war, conflict, sexual desire and Gothic romance. It was a world that continued to consume her imagination well into her twenties.

Many of these stories survive today and, collectively, they amount to more words than the novels of Charlotte, Anne and Emily put together.[2] The stories, especially those written in the late 1820s and early 1830s, are infused with a kind of fantasy realism that brings together magical and paranormal forces with a sometimes brutal authenticity. Think *Game of Thrones*, but with less nudity.

The imaginative potential of the supernatural was not lost on Charlotte and her siblings. As we'll see, it features heavily in the Glass Town and Angrian tales of their younger years – but it also appears in the later works, particularly *Jane Eyre* and *Villette*, and Emily's *Wuthering Heights* (Anne's novels are comparatively much more down to earth). Despite Charlotte's renunciation of these fantastical worlds at the age of twenty-three, she returned again and again to similar themes, as a means of expanding the horizons of her books and of highlighting the slim psychological line between reality and fantasy, sanity and instability. The playful possibilities of magic in her youthful work formed the foundations of her mature writing, in which the paranormal and the uncanny became the more nuanced and effective instruments adopted.

People are drawn to the inexplicable. The supernatural allows us to explore uncharted territory within ourselves and the ongoing (dare I say, endless?) obsession with werewolves, zombies and vampires goes to show that we still rely on alternative universes to answer deep questions about our lives. With this in mind, I'm going to consider the scary and supernatural side to Charlotte's work and see how closely linked it is to the genres of fantasy and magical realism as depicted in the 21st century.

FANTASY WORLDS

The young Brontë siblings' imaginary world of violence, passion and magical mischief all began with twelve toy soldiers, which Charlotte wrote about on 12 March 1829 in a piece titled 'The History of the Year':

> Papa bought Branwell some soldiers at Leeds. When Papa came home it was night and we were in bed, so next morning Branwell came to our door with a box of soldiers. Emily and I jumped out of bed and I snatched up one and exclaimed, 'This is the Duke of Wellington! It shall be mine!' When I said this, Emily likewise took one and said it should be hers. When Anne came down she took one also. Mine was the prettiest of the whole and perfect in every part. Emily's was a grave-looking fellow. We called him Gravey. Anne's was a queer little thing, very much like herself. He was called Waiting Boy. Branwell chose Bonaparte.[3]

This is the beginning of their Young Men's 'plays' together, set in the imaginary and imaginative realm of the Glass Town Federation (later known as the Verdopolitan Union). Located

Toy figures: staples of the 19th-century imagination.

around the delta of the River Niger, most likely in Ghana, the city of Great Glass Town (later known as Verreopolis and then Verdopolis) was founded by a motley crew of Englishmen, one of whom would go on to become the Duke of Wellington. I say 'founded', but really the land was forcefully taken from the Kingdom of Ashantee, based on the real Kingdom of Ashanti of the 18th and 19th centuries. (More on Charlotte's iffy imperialism in the next chapter.)

The twelve soldiers conquered the territory and four magical Chief Genii – the supernatural alter-egos of Anne, Branwell, Charlotte, and Emily – oversaw the building of their city. But it was a far from straightforward task, as this excerpt from 'The Twelve Adventurers' (15 April 1829) shows:

> About a month after we had begun our city the following adventure happened to us.
>
> One evening when all were assembled in the great tent, and most of us sitting round the fire which blazed in the middle of the pavilion, listening to the storm which raged without our camp, a dead silence prevailed. None of us felt inclined to speak, still less to laugh, and the wine-cups stood upon the round table filled to the brim. In the midst of this silence we heard the sound of a trumpet, which seemed to come from the desert. The next moment a peal of thunder rolled through the sky, which seemed to shake the earth to its centre.
>
> By this time we were all on our legs and filled with terror, which was changed to desperation by another blast of the terrible trumpet. We all rushed out of the tent with a shout, not of courage, but fear, and then we saw a sight so terribly grand that even now when I think of it, at the distance of forty years from that dismal night when I saw it, my limbs tremble and my blood is chilled

with fear. High in the clouds was a tall and terrible giant. In his right hand he held a trumpet, in his left, two darts pointed with fire. On a thunder cloud which rolled before him his shield rested. On his forehead was written 'The Genius of the Storm'. On he strode over the black clouds which rolled beneath his feet and regardless of the fierce lightning which flashed around him. But soon the thunder ceased and the lightning no longer glared so terribly.

The hoarse voice of the storm was hushed, and a gentler light than the fire of the elements spread itself over the face of the now cloudless sky. The calm moon shone forth in the midst of the firmament, and the little stars seemed rejoicing in their brightness. The giant had descended to the earth, and, approaching the place where we stood trembling, he made three circles in the air with his flaming scimitar, then lifted his hand to strike. Just then we heard a loud voice saying, 'Genius, I command thee to forbear!'

We looked round and saw a figure so tall that the Genius seemed to it but a diminutive dwarf. It cast one joyful glance on us and disappeared.[4]

Amidst all the hilarity and drama, Charlotte – at the age of twelve – proves herself already aware of the nuances of narrative voice and of the self-conscious role of the omniscient author. Her Genii, called Tallii, takes on Branwell's power-hungry 'Genius of the Storm' in a bid to regain control of her narrative. Not only does Tallii's intervention put Branwell in his place; it also allows Charlotte to explore different ways for the authorial voice to break into the story, a technique that she used vividly in *Jane Eyre*. In her magical Genii persona, we see the beginnings of Charlotte's literary genius. We see her funny side, too. After all, the supernatural is meant to be fantastical

Violent scenes in a Victorian penny dreadful.

and unbelievable, a force that shatters reality. In her younger years, this was exactly what Charlotte depicted in her writing.

All of these elements – the battles and violence, the humour and the supernatural forces – mean the young Brontës' sagas are an ancestor of the hugely popular HBO series, *Game of Thrones*, based on the George R. R. Martin *A Song of Ice and Fire* novels. The premise of both is similar: various figureheads – some magical, some mortal – are vying for power and are willing to use brute force, violence and dark magic to come out on top. There is also the fact that both narratives and their various family trees are intricately complex and, at times, hard to follow. The similarities between the two are numerous, but the Brontës started their saga between the ages of eleven and seven and they did not have a mega budget with CGI dragons. There were no televisions or cinemas to feed their literary imaginations; books like the *Arabian Nights* were their evening entertainment. That's not to criticise George R. R. Martin – he and the HBO team have created a spectacle of ingenuity. It's more to point out how remarkable it is that four young siblings created such a complicated and bloody realm from nothing more than twelve toy soldiers, a back catalogue of previously read stories, and their own vibrant imaginations.

It has been argued that Charlotte and her siblings used their stories not only as an expression of silly sibling rivalry, but as a means of control.[5] After the deaths of their mother and two elder sisters, the Brontë children sought refuge in their writing and, in the face of death and illness, they saw their imaginary

Arabian Nights (Dalziel illustration).

worlds as places to conquer and control. Magic plays a big part in this desire for power.[6] It can act as an irrepressible force that must be obeyed; it can both restore and devastate with the swipe of a hand:

> Sir – it is well known that the Genii have declared that unless they 'perform certain arduous duties every year, of a mysterious nature, all the worlds in the firmament will be burnt up and gathered together in one mighty globe, which will roll in lonely grandeur through the vast wilderness of space, inhabited only by the four high Princes of the Genii, till time shall be succeeded by eternity'. The impudence of this is only to be paralleled by another of their assertions, namely, 'that by their magic might they can reduce [sic] the world to a desert, the rivers to streams of livid poison and the clearest lakes to stagnant waters, the pestilential vapours of which shall slay all living creatures, except the blood-thirsty beast of the forest and the ravenous bird of the rock. But that in the midst of this desolation the Palace of the Chief Genii shall rise sparkling in the wilderness, and the horrible howl of their war-cry shall spread over the land at morning, at noontide and night; but that they shall have their annual feast over the bones of the dead and shall yearly rejoice with the joy of victors.' I think, sir, that the horrible wickedness of this needs no remark, and therefore I haste to subscribe myself, yours etc.,
>
> *UT*

Charlotte, alongside Branwell ('UT' means 'us two', which suggests they probably both had a hand in composing this fragment), paints a pretty violent picture in this 'letter' from 14 July 1829.[7] Magic is the main weapon wielded, but there's

The Duke of Wellington: his son inspired the Brontës' fantasy world.

also something biblical in what the Chief Genii are threatening, like the plagues of Egypt. In the early years of their fictional world, Charlotte and her siblings are all-powerful. Thanks to their supernatural guises, they are gods. Considering this was the early 19th century, a time when religion affected almost every aspect of existence in Britain, the self-conscious decision to embody explicitly omnipotent beings in their fiction is extraordinary.

Over time, the Chief Genii were relegated to the outskirts of the fictional realm, particularly as the stories' focus became directed at the city of Angria instead of Glass Town. Charlotte chose the sardonic voice of Charles Townshend (formerly Wellesley, based on one of the real-life sons of the Duke of Wellington) as the narrator of most of her Angrian tales and, from his ironic – and notably male – perspective, followed the illicit Byronic ways of his brother, the Duke of Zamorna, another fictionalised son of Wellington. In 1831, Charlotte wrote the poem 'The trumpet hath sounded', in which the four Chief Genii – Tallii, Branii, Emmii, and Annii – were banished from the saga:

… The hall where they sat was the heart of the sky
And the stars to give light stooped their lamps from on high
The noise of the host rose like thunder around
The heavens gathered gloom at the hoarse sullen sound
No mortal may farther the vision reveal
Human eye cannot peirce [*sic*] what a spirit could seal
The secrets of Genii my tongue may not tell
But hoarsely they murmured bright city farewell
Then melted away like a dream of the night
While their palace evanished in oceans of light …[8]

Magic was eventually sidelined for romance in Charlotte's affections. Yet this wasn't the end of the supernatural in her work. It acted as a base upon which she built her later novels, which were each infused with a darkness and an uncanniness indebted to her Genii adventures.

MAGICAL MYTHS & GRUESOME FAIRYTALES

The Gytrash

In *Jane Eyre*, magical myths feature heavily in Jane and Mr Rochester's relationship. In their first meeting, both mistake the other for an otherworldly spirit. While walking to the village of Hay to post a letter, a solitary Jane hears the stamp of a horse's hooves and is convinced that it is the Gytrash, a mythical animal spirit (usually a dog or a horse) she was told about as a young girl. Think of Sirius Black's Patronus, 'Padfoot', in J.K. Rowling's *Harry Potter and the Prisoner of Azkaban*, and you will have a pretty accurate image of a Gytrash.

When Rochester's dog, Pilot, makes an appearance, Jane is further persuaded that she is being visited by the strange creature. Then Rochester rides into view and Jane's own eerie presence is enough to startle both the horse and the rider:

> A rude noise broke on these fine ripplings and whisperings, at once so far away and so clear: a positive tramp, tramp, a metallic clatter, which effaced the soft wave-wanderings; as, in a picture, the solid mass of a crag, or the rough boles of a great oak, drawn in dark and strong on the foreground, efface the aërial distance of azure hill, sunny horizon, and blended clouds where tint melts into tint.
>
> The din was on the causeway: a horse was coming; the windings of the lane yet hid it, but it approached. I was just leaving the stile; yet, as the path was narrow, I sat still to let it go by. In those days I was young, and all sorts of fancies bright and dark tenanted my mind: the memories of nursery stories were there amongst other rubbish; and when they recurred, maturing youth added to them a vigour and vividness beyond what childhood could give. As this horse approached, and as I watched for it to appear through the dusk, I remembered certain of Bessie's tales, wherein figured a North-of-England spirit called a 'Gytrash,' which, in the form of horse, mule, or large dog, haunted solitary ways, and sometimes came upon belated travellers, as this horse was now coming upon me.
>
> It was very near, but not yet in sight; when, in addition to the tramp, tramp, I heard a rush under the hedge, and close down by the hazel stems glided a great dog, whose black and white colour made him a distinct object against the trees. It was exactly one form of

The Gytrash - illustration by F.H. Townsend.

Bessie's Gytrash—a lion-like creature with long hair and a huge head: it passed me, however, quietly enough; not staying to look up, with strange pretercanine eyes, in my face, as I half expected it would. The horse followed, —a tall steed, and on its back a rider. The man, the human being, broke the spell at once. Nothing ever rode the Gytrash: it was always alone; and goblins, to my notions, though they might tenant the dumb carcasses of beasts, could scarce covet shelter in the commonplace human form. No Gytrash was this, —only a traveller taking the short cut to Millcote. He passed, and I went on; a few steps, and I turned: a sliding sound and an exclamation of "What the deuce is to do now?" and a clattering tumble, arrested my attention. Man and horse were down; they had slipped on the sheet of ice which glazed the

causeway. The dog came bounding back, and seeing his master in a predicament, and hearing the horse groan, barked till the evening hills echoed the sound, which was deep in proportion to his magnitude.[9]

In many ways, Jane's imagined Gytrash is a warning. Something changeable and unknown is approaching, and Jane tries to make sense of the impending vision by defaulting to her childhood. As with the Brontë children's attempts to gain control over their lives through their fictional magical world, Jane's Gytrash is an effort to make sense of what's coming next. Even though she is wrong in her anticipatory assumption, she prepares herself for the unexpected and what she in fact encounters is perhaps stranger than a creature from a folktale.

Rochester does not declare himself as Jane's employer at this point, preferring to interrogate her while remaining a stranger. Their relationship begins with mystery and myth, then, which only intensifies throughout their flirtatious and often combative encounters. Jane is susceptible to fanciful folklore and superstition, embellishing what otherwise might have been a pretty normal meeting with magic. It's worth remembering that Jane is only eighteen years old when she meets Rochester. Barely out of childhood, the first thing she thinks of when she hears a horse approaching on a dark road is mythical stories.

Yet Rochester is also a fan of spirits, particularly in relation to Jane herself. He repeatedly calls Jane 'spirit' and, having revealed that he is in fact her boss, he likens her to 'the men in green', otherwise known as elves:

'[…] And so you were waiting for your people when you sat on that stile?'

'For whom, sir?'

'For the men in green: it was a proper moonlight evening for them. Did I break through one of your rings, that you spread that damned ice on the causeway?'

I shook my head. 'The men in green all forsook England a hundred years ago,' said I, speaking as seriously as he had done. 'And not even in Hay Lane, or the fields about it, could you find a trace of them. I don't think either summer or harvest, or winter moon, will ever shine on their revels more.'

Mrs Fairfax had dropped her knitting, and, with raised eyebrows, seemed wondering what sort of talk this was.[10]

As a means of understanding their unpredictable encounter, and perhaps their strange attraction to each other, they resort to mythical and magical explanations. These forces continue to influence the development of their relationship, punctuating Charlotte's narrative and changing the direction of the novel. The lingering sense of Rochester and his animals as a kind of Gytrash, something elusive and threatening but ultimately deficient in the power he represents (as shown by his falling on the ice), is sustained throughout most of the book. There is something unattainable about him, which the reader (and Jane) soon discovers to be his wife, Bertha, in the attic.

But there is also an odd vulnerability to him, a neediness that borders on violence at times. If he does not get what he wants, such as marriage to Jane, he becomes incandescently angry. When Bertha's existence is revealed to Jane, Rochester refuses to accept that she cannot live with him as his mistress at the very least; when she resists his attempts to cajole her into this fate, he threatens rape. In many respects, he acts as an over-grown man-child incapable of facing up to his errors and frequent immorality. This is contrary to the popular perception of his character as a romantic hero, the man of your dreams. He is not a bad man, necessarily; and there is something strangely alluring about his mystery and vulnerability. But he is by no means a masculine ideal.

Looking beyond he and Jane's intense connection, which is what many women (and men) find so appealing, Rochester is deeply flawed and requires salvation. The spell of Rochester as the enigmatic, brooding and romantic man is shattered not only when he slips on the ice, but repeatedly throughout *Jane Eyre*.

Cinderella in the Red Room

Jane Eyre is a classic rags-to-riches tale. It is unsurprising, then, that it shares several similarities with *Cinderella*, the prototype of that genre and still a hugely popular story today, not least in pantomimes and films, as well as in children's bedtime books. Jane is an orphan and spends much of her early life in a big house with her evil aunt and selfish cousins. She is an ill-treated outcast without much hope for the future, even once she settles in at Lowood School. It is her own initiative and determination that move her up in the world (as well as rather conveniently inheriting a large sum of money from her long-lost uncle in Madeira, but the shoe still fits). From the beginning, we are rooting for Jane to triumph morally and socially over all those who disregard her. In the end, she succeeds and gets her happy ending: reader, she marries him.

It is the cruelty of her aunt and cousins that initially highlights the Cinderella pattern in the novel. At Gateshead, her aunt's home, Jane is relegated to a second-class citizen. She is abused verbally and physically, made to feel unloved and unwanted. After a particularly bloody spat with her cousin,

John Reed (who hits Jane over the head with a book, thus forcing her to hit him in return), she is sent as punishment to the red room, the bedroom in which her kind uncle, Mr Reed, died:

The red-room was a square chamber, very seldom slept in, I might say never, indeed, unless when a chance influx of visitors at Gateshead Hall rendered it necessary to turn to account all the accommodation it contained: yet it was one of the largest and stateliest chambers in the mansion. A bed supported on massive pillars of mahogany, hung with curtains of deep red damask, stood out like a tabernacle in the centre; the two large windows, with their blinds always drawn down, were half shrouded in festoons and falls of similar drapery; the carpet was red; the table at the foot of the bed was covered with a crimson cloth; the walls were a soft fawn colour with a blush of pink in it; the wardrobe, the toilet-table, the chairs were of darkly polished old mahogany. Out of these deep surrounding shades rose high, and glared white, the piled-up mattresses and pillows of the bed, spread with a snowy Marseilles counterpane. Scarcely less prominent was an ample cushioned easy-chair near the head of the bed, also white, with a footstool before it; and looking, as I thought, like a pale throne.

> This room was chill, because it seldom had a fire; it was silent, because remote from the nursery and kitchen; solemn, because it was known to be so seldom entered. The house-maid alone came here on Saturdays, to wipe from the mirrors and the furniture a week's quiet dust: and Mrs. Reed herself, at far intervals, visited it to review the contents of a certain secret drawer in the wardrobe, where were stored divers parchments, her jewel-casket, and a miniature of her deceased husband; and in those last words lies the secret of the red-room— the spell which kept it so lonely in spite of its grandeur.
>
> Mr. Reed had been dead nine years: it was in this chamber he breathed his last; here he lay in state; hence his coffin was borne by the undertaker's men; and, since that day, a sense of dreary consecration had guarded it from frequent intrusion.[11]

The red room has become a place where Mrs Reed can store her husband's belongings and his memory. It is untouched, almost forgotten, but there is not the sense that this is out of respect for the dead. If Mrs Reed holds the room in high esteem, as a consecrated space in which she can peacefully mourn her husband, her decision to throw her niece in there as a chastisement is a strange one. Why the red room?

Well, for one, it is probably haunted. Jane's aunt may not have seen Mr Reed's ghost in the room, but she clearly knew the power of that space and its lingering presence of death. This knowledge of the room's possible spiritual energy no doubt influenced Mrs Reed when making her choice of punishment. Send Jane to the red room and let her imagination run wild:

A singular notion dawned upon me. I doubted not—never doubted—that if Mr. Reed had been alive he would have treated me kindly; and now, as I sat looking at the white bed and overshadowed walls—occasionally also turning a fascinated eye towards the dimly gleaning mirror—I began to recall what I had heard of dead men, troubled in their graves by the violation of their last wishes, revisiting the earth to punish the perjured and avenge the oppressed; and I thought Mr. Reed's spirit, harassed by the wrongs of his sister's child, might quit its abode—whether in the church vault or in the unknown world of the departed—and rise before me in this chamber. I wiped my tears and hushed my sobs, fearful lest any sign of violent grief might waken a preternatural voice to comfort me, or elicit from the gloom some haloed face, bending over me with strange pity. This idea, consolatory in theory, I felt would be terrible if realised: with all my might I endeavoured to stifle it—I endeavoured to be firm. Shaking my hair from my eyes, I lifted my head and tried to look boldly round the dark room; at this moment a light gleamed on the wall. Was it, I asked myself, a ray from the moon penetrating some aperture in the blind? No; moonlight was still, and this stirred; while I gazed, it glided up to the ceiling and quivered over my head. I can now conjecture readily that this streak of light was, in all likelihood, a gleam from a lantern carried by some one across the lawn: but then, prepared as my mind was for horror, shaken as my nerves were by agitation, I thought the swift darting beam was a herald of some coming vision from another world. My heart beat thick, my head grew hot; a sound filled my ears, which I deemed the rushing of wings; something seemed near me; I was oppressed, suffocated: endurance

> broke down; I rushed to the door and shook the lock in desperate effort. Steps came running along the outer passage; the key turned, Bessie and Abbot entered.[12]

Jane's distress is dismissed by her aunt, however, who pushes her back into the red room and locks the door. She falls unconscious through terror and wakes up in her own bed surrounded by a doctor and Bessie. It is a formative moment in Jane's life. The injustice of her treatment, its inexplicable cruelty, strengthens her own sense of self-worth. Instead of breaking Jane, her supernatural encounter reinforces her determination to seek a better world.

Once again, the supernatural plays a decisive role in the direction of Jane's life. Just as Disney's Cinderella has a fairy godmother to transform her (superficially), Jane also has her own spiritual overseers. The only difference – and it is a major one – is that none of the magical forces that lead to Cinderella marrying the handsome prince are within her control. The spiritual visions in *Jane Eyre* all stem from Jane's own imagination. She believes she sees her uncle's ghost; she hears the Gytrash and, later, Rochester's voice on the wind; she resembles an otherworldly fairy. It all comes from her, no one else. She does not have a kind fairy godmother to dress her in exquisite gowns or get her to the ball on time (Rochester definitely doesn't count). And although her other uncle from Madeira leaves her a substantial inheritance, by that time, Jane's own sense of self is strong enough for the reader to know that she will prevail – penniless or not.

Bertha and Bluebeard

The author John Sutherland has already alerted readers of *Jane Eyre* to its parallels with the French folktale about Bluebeard, or *La Barbe bleue*.[13] In his tongue-in-cheek article, Sutherland fears for Jane's safety once she and Rochester are married. After all, this is the same man who locked his wife in an attic and blamed everyone but himself for her eventual death. Beneath the article's facetious veneer, however, there is the more unsettling suggestion that Rochester could turn murderous.

Bluebeard is a rich, middle-aged man whose distinctive facial hair leaves women cold. Despite his unattractive appearance, he has had several wives, all of whom have vanished mysteriously. Having remarried, he goes away on a trip, leaving his wife in the chateau; before he leaves, he presents her with the keys to the castle, telling her to explore all of its riches. There is just one room he forbids her from entering. Of course, she disobeys and unlocks the door. Inside are the bodies of her husband's previous wives, hanging from the wall. In her shock, she drops the key in the blood; typically, it stains and when Bluebeard returns early, he notices the blood and knows what his wife has found. She must die. Thankfully, her brothers save the day by killing Bluebeard. He gets his comeuppance and his surviving wife inherits his wealth.

As Sutherland points out, there are quite a few overlaps between this Bluebeard character and our very own Mr Rochester. For one thing, he was never a looker. Michael Fassbender and Toby Stephens make convincingly brooding Rochesters, but they also embody the more romanticised, fantasised version of him: mysterious but sexy. A bit like Colin Firth's Darcy. Charlotte's Rochester is rude, moody and (even according to Jane) ugly. And he also has a secret wife locked in his attic:

In a room without a window, there burnt a fire guarded by a high and strong fender, and a lamp suspended from the ceiling by a chain. Grace Poole bent over the fire, apparently cooking something in a saucepan. In the deep shade, at the farther end of the room, a figure ran backwards and forwards. What it was, whether beast or human being, one could not, at first sight, tell: it grovelled, seemingly, on all fours; it snatched and growled like some strange wild animal: but it was covered with clothing, and a quantity of dark, grizzled hair, wild as a mane, hid its head and face [...]

Mr. Rochester flung me behind him: the lunatic sprang and grappled his throat viciously, and laid her teeth to his cheek: they struggled. She was a big woman, in stature almost equalling her husband, and corpulent besides: she showed virile force in the contest— more than once she almost throttled him, athletic as he was. He could have settled her with a well-planted blow; but he would not strike: he would only wrestle. At last he mastered her arms; Grace Poole gave him a cord, and he pinioned them behind her: with more rope, which was at hand, he bound her to a chair. The operation was performed amidst the fiercest yells and the most convulsive plunges. Mr. Rochester then turned to the spectators: he looked at them with a smile both acrid and desolate.

'That is *my wife*,' said he. 'Such is the sole conjugal embrace I am ever to know—such are the endearments which are to solace my leisure hours! And *this* is what I wished to have' (laying his hand on my shoulder): 'this young girl, who stands so grave and quiet at the mouth of hell, looking collectedly at the gambols of a demon, I wanted her just as a change after that fierce ragout. Wood and Briggs, look at the difference! Compare these clear eyes with the red balls yonder—this face with that mask—this form with that bulk; then judge me, priest of the gospel and man of the law, and remember with what judgment ye judge ye shall be judged! Off with you now. I must shut up my prize.'[14]

Bertha is likened to an animal, an object ('my prize'), and a vampire, trying to draw blood from her victim. Before this encounter, she bit her own brother. There is also a touch of the Gytrash about her, with her long dark 'mane' and unpredictability. Whatever she resembles, she does not appear to be of this world. She is characterised completely as the 'Other'.

Vampire stories were as popular in the 19th century as today.

Rochester's crimes are not quite as grotesque as Bluebeard's and he does seek repentance from his past sins. Yet he never takes responsibility for the treatment or fate of Bertha; he hates her and wishes her dead. When she does die, falling from the top of Thornfield away from the flames of her own making – and also escaping from Rochester, presumably – he is not blamed. He is pitied and Bertha goes unmourned. Sutherland has a point. Perhaps Rochester was a distant relation of Bluebeard. Not quite a criminal, but still guilty.

A tapestry of fairytales makes up *Jane Eyre*, with countless allusions to folklore both deliberate and accidental woven through its narrative. Perhaps this is why William Thackeray, upon first reading the novel, wrote that the 'plot of the story is one with wh[ich], I am familiar'.[15] It also partly accounts for the book's enduring nature, its fixity in our literary lexicon. Fairytales, superstitions and myths are part of our everyday cultural thought processes, whether we recognise it or not. The prince charmings, the evil mothers-in-law or aunts, the woman in the attic, the luck or bad luck of seeing a black animal: in one form or another, these are all tropes that make up our language in newspapers, on television and down the pub. And they are all – again, in one form or another – reworked and re-imagined in Charlotte's *Jane Eyre*.

GOTHICISM & *VILLETTE*

Sex and violence are two sides of the same coin in Gothicism. Beneath the exhilarating and romantic mask of the grand manor in classic gothic fiction lurks the possibility of violence and the inevitability of death. Readers gain a strange pleasure from imagining the swooning and the horror, the delicious nonsense of it all. Charlotte enjoyed gothic writing, especially that of Sir Walter Scott, her hero of prose, with all of his Scottish

Castles, dungeons, always on dark nights...

castles and sublime landscapes. It is also likely that she came across Ann Radcliffe, the mother of gothic fiction, in the circulating libraries, particularly when you consider the themes of female incarceration and entrapment that emerge in both Radcliffe and Charlotte's fiction.

And then, of course, there was Byron with his languid debauchery and the dark myths that surrounded his biography. He also instigated the ghost story competition that led to Mary Shelley's dreaming the origins of *Frankenstein* (1818). Charlotte's respect for the genre filtered into her own work and she borrowed – consciously or otherwise – several key elements from Gothicism. The supernatural is one such aspect, as quintessential to the gothic mode as sex, violence and castles.

Every haunted house had its own ghostly legends.

In Charlotte's third published novel, *Villette*, the ghost of a nun is introduced as a means of emphasising Lucy Snowe's isolation from the world and from her own identity, as well as feeding into the tradition of the bleeding nun, as seen in Matthew Lewis's classic 1796 novel, *The Monk*. Initially, the nun is explained as a haunted house story, in which the boarding school where Lucy teaches and lives was the location of an unknown, but presumably gruesome, incident:

> There went a tradition that Madame Beck's house had in old days been a convent. That in years gone by—how long gone by I cannot tell, but I think some centuries—before the city had over-spread this quarter, and when it was tilled ground and avenue, and such deep and leafy seclusion as ought to embosom a religious house-that something had happened on this site which, rousing fear

and inflicting horror, had left to the place the inheritance of a ghost-story. A vague tale went of a black and white nun, sometimes, on some night or nights of the year, seen in some part of this vicinage. The ghost must have been built out some ages ago, for there were houses all round now; but certain convent-relics, in the shape of old and huge fruit-trees, yet consecrated the spot; and, at the foot of one—a Methuselah of a pear-tree, dead, all but a few boughs which still faithfully renewed their perfumed snow in spring, and their honey-sweet pendants in autumn—you saw, in scraping away the mossy earth between the half-bared roots, a glimpse of slab, smooth, hard, and black. The legend went, unconfirmed and unaccredited, but still propagated, that this was the portal of a vault, imprisoning deep beneath that ground, on whose surface grass grew and flowers bloomed, the bones of a girl whom a monkish conclave of the drear middle ages had here buried alive for some sin against her vow. Her shadow it was that tremblers had feared, through long generations after her poor frame was dust; her black robe and white veil that, for timid eyes, moonlight and shade had mocked, as they fluctuated in the night-wind through the garden-thicket.

Independently of romantic rubbish, however, that old garden had its charms. On summer mornings I used to rise early, to enjoy them alone; on summer evenings, to linger solitary, to keep tryste with the rising moon, or taste one kiss of the evening breeze, or fancy rather than feel the freshness of dew descending. The turf was verdant, the gravelled walks were white; sun-bright nasturtiums clustered beautiful about the roots of the doddered orchard giants. There was a large berceau, above which spread the shade of an acacia; there was a smaller, more

sequestered bower, nestled in the vines which ran all
along a high and grey wall, and gathered their tendrils in
a knot of beauty, and hung their clusters in loving profu-
sion about the favoured spot where jasmine and ivy met
and married them.[16]

Despite, or predictably because of, dismissing the tale as
'romantic rubbish' (Charlotte was adept in simultaneously mock-
ing and embracing the sensational elements of the gothic), Lucy
encounters the ghastly nun on several occasions. As someone
prone to depression and extreme loneliness, the solid-looking
spectre acts as a projection of Lucy's status as an outsider, as well
as her own inner psychological battles:

> If life be a war, it seemed my destiny to conduct it sin-
> gle-handed. I pondered now how to break up my win-
> ter-quarters—to leave an encampment where food and
> forage failed. Perhaps, to effect this change, another
> pitched battle must be fought with fortune; if so, I had
> a mind to the encounter: too poor to lose, God might
> destine me to gain. But what road was open?—what plan
> available?
>
> On this question I was still pausing, when the moon, so
> dim hitherto, seemed to shine out somewhat brighter: a
> ray even gleamed white before me, and a shadow became
> distinct and marked. I looked more narrowly, to make
> out the cause of this well-defined contrast appearing a
> little suddenly in the obscure alley: whiter and blacker it
> grew on my eye: it took shape with instantaneous trans-
> formation. I stood about three yards from a tall, sable-
> robed, snowy-veiled woman.
>
> Five minutes passed. I neither fled nor shrieked. She
> was there still. I spoke.

'Who are you? and why do you come to me?'

She stood mute. She had no face—no features: all below her brow was masked with a white cloth; but she had eyes, and they viewed me.

I felt, if not brave, yet a little desperate; and desperation will often suffice to fill the post and do the work of courage. I advanced one step. I stretched out my hand, for I meant to touch her. She seemed to recede. I drew nearer: her recession, still silent, became swift. A mass of shrubs, full-leaved evergreens—laurel and dense yew— intervened between me and what I followed. Having passed that obstacle, I looked and saw nothing. I waited. I said,—'If you have any errand to me, come back and deliver it.' Nothing spoke or re-appeared.

This time there was no Dr. John to whom to have recourse: there was no one to whom I dared whisper the words, 'I have again seen the nun.'[17]

The skeleton of a nun – she haunts the building.

A proper gothic faint.

Lucy has no one to confide in about her vision. Seeing the ghostly nun heightens her sense of loneliness, her total isolation from love and companionship. This is emphasised further when the nun's identity is posited as that of Justine Marie, the woman whom Monsieur Paul Emanuel (Lucy's would-be lover) was apparently in love with as a young man. When they were unable to marry, Justine Marie fled to a convent where she later died. Paul Emanuel then took a vow of chastity, which makes the possibility of he and Lucy getting together a bit tricky. Justine Marie as the ghostly nun acts as an 'eternal barrier' between them, then; and her apparent haunting of Lucy is therefore a smug reminder of the happiness she will never gain.

As with most supernatural occurrences in Charlotte's writing, as well as in the majority of (female) gothic fiction, there is a simple explanation to the apparition. It is merely one of Lucy's pupils, the flighty Ginevra Fanshawe, sneaking her boyfriend in and out of the school. This explanation still casts doubts over Lucy's frame of mind: would a white sheet thrown over a grown man really convince you that he is really a ghost? Not likely. But it is an example of what Charlotte does so well, embellishing reality with the spectres of our own conjuring and reminding readers that so much of what we see and feel is imagined or invisible. She fully utilises the power of the gothic to make a point about perceptions of the female psyche as hysterical and prone to hallucinations, not simply as a means of raising the reader's heart rate.

Even in the 21st century, we're still seeing the ripple effect of Gothicism, particularly onscreen. Guillermo del Toro's film, *Crimson Peak*, was released in 2015 and has all the markers of a traditional gothic tale. There's the big, crumbling stately home, which just happens to be sinking into the blood red soil on which it stands; the complicated family history of the Sharps; a major secret that is hinted at throughout to build suspense; and then there's the sex, ghosts and violence. Of course, as we have seen, *Jane Eyre* (and to a lesser extent, *Villette*) has all of this, too, and it's telling (though unsurprising) that *Crimson Peak* has been associated with the Brontës in several reviews, with one even explicitly titling itself 'Guillermo del Toro's *Crimson Peak* is a delicious Bronte stew' [sic].[18] *Jane Eyre* is undoubtedly one of – if not *the* – best known gothic romances in English literature, so any new cinematic additions to the genre will inevitably come up against Charlotte's novel.

What is surprising, however, is how little the adaptations and popular perceptions of *Jane Eyre* acknowledge its gothic overtones. The red room scene, the encounter with the 'Gytrash', and the disturbing presence of Bertha Mason (mainly, for modern audiences, because we feel uncomfortable about her ill treatment) could all make for shocking and unsettling viewing. There is darkness in the recent and not-so recent adaptations, particularly Orson Welles' gruff Rochester from 1943 and the shaky camera focus in Carey Fukunaga's 2011 *Jane Eyre*. But none of these films emphasise the truly troubling subtext of Charlotte's novel. There needs to be a supernatural revolutionising of *Jane Eyre*, one that destabilises its characterisation as a commonplace romance and instead gives due weight to the myth, fairytale and Gothicism at the centre of the story. Charlotte deserves no less.

FIVE

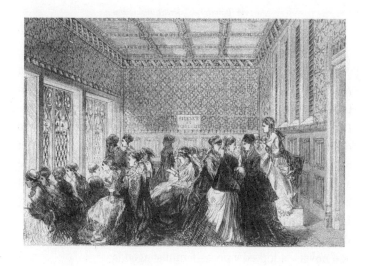

CHARLOTTE
AND IDEOLOGY

Above: 'bewitched', irrational women.
Previous page: Ladies' Gallery, House of Commons.

Considering the radical subject matter of Charlotte's novels, it is unsurprising that she has regularly been painted as a revolutionary. *Jane Eyre* was one of the first books to give an introspective account of a child's life from a child's perspective, and a girl-child, at that! The directness and dominance of Jane's voice – her demand for more – was unprecedented at a time when women were marginalised in society. Charlotte also frequently wrote from a male point of view, a device that enabled her to explore less 'ladylike' aspects of human nature. In *Villette*, she dealt with themes of sexuality and mental breakdown with explicit intensity. And *Shirley* – her only third-person novel – adopted a proto-feminist agenda.

Yet there was also a more traditionalist side to Charlotte. She was not an outright supporter of women gaining the vote. She was not a pacifist – at least, not as a child. She was a traditionalist Tory supporter. She found the idea of writing overtly about politics and religion distasteful (even though she did so). By our comparatively more liberal 21st-century standards, some of Charlotte's beliefs can be hard to square with her literary radicalism.

Like most people, Charlotte does not easily fit into a single box: she can't really be characterised as 'left' or 'right', 'progressive' or 'conformist'. Her opinions cannot be divided up and then neatly labelled, and it would be overly simplistic to condense her outlook into a simple dichotomy.

Part of Charlotte's appeal lies in her contradictions, which we can trace through her letters and in her novels. She may have harboured an early interest in the French Revolution and Napoleon Bonaparte, and a love of Lord Byron, the poster-boy of transgression. But she also had a lifelong fascination with the Duke of Wellington, the two-time Tory Prime Minister, military hero of Waterloo and fierce critic of political reform. Even in *Shirley*, published in 1849 when she was thirty-three, Charlotte was still defending Arthur Wellesley:

> Men of Manchester! [...] Lord Wellington is, for you, only a decayed old gentleman now: I rather think some of you have called him a 'dotard' – you have taunted him with his age, and the loss of his physical vigour. What fine heroes you are yourselves! Men like you have a right to trample on what is mortal in a demigod. Scoff at your ease – your scorn can never break his grand, old heart.[1]

Scenes from the French Revolution were widely circulated.

This mix of the conservative and the rebellious, the conformist and the sensational is the backbone of Charlotte's writing and a crucial means of placing her novels in their historical context.

There is a danger in judging the past by the standards of the present. The word 'problematic' is bandied around frequently and has become almost a cliché in Internet circles because so much is problematic, especially when it originated in the 19th century. We cannot expect Charlotte or her novels to represent our society completely. When I question her conservatism or her feminism, it is my own reservations with which I am wrestling. It is not about Charlotte's 'failings' or imperfections, or even a case of agreeing or disagreeing with her. It is more a case of seeing ourselves in relation to Charlotte Brontë, as this chapter aims to achieve.

A POLITICAL ANIMAL?

Tory Leanings

Charlotte and her siblings were voracious readers from an early age. Although their home library was relatively small (Patrick Brontë had a modest salary and books were expensive), the family had other ways of consuming stories. The various lending libraries that passed through Haworth was one source, but the newspapers that Patrick brought into the house had a particularly noticeable impact on his children's literary imaginations.

In 'The History of the Year', which chronicles the beginnings of the siblings' literary plays, Charlotte dedicates a full paragraph to the various newspapers and magazines entering the parsonage:

Papa and Branwell are gone for the newspaper, the *Leeds Intelligencer*, a most excellent Tory news paper edited by Mr [Edwa]rd Wood [for] the proprietor Mr Hernaman. We take 2 and see three newspapers a week. We take the *Leeds Intelligencer*, party Tory, and the *Leeds Mercury*, Whig, edited by Mr Baines and his brother, son in law and his 2 sons, Edward and Talbot. We see the *John Bull*; it is a High Tory, very violent. Mr Driver lends us it, as likewise *Blackwood's Magazine*, the most able periodical there is.[2]

Charlotte wrote this when she was just twelve years old. By that age, she was already familiar with political allegiances and divisions, and even the sometimes subtle differences between a generically Tory paper and a more virulent one. Her early awareness of political factions, and all the drama that ensued, shaped the progression of her youthful writing and ultimately her later novels.

'Integrity retiring from office', 1801: a Whigs/Tories standoff.

Tories in the 21st century are a little different to their 19th-century equivalents, though they are both accurately characterised by their conservative outlook. The late 18th-century and early 19th-century party (led by William Pitt from 1783), which we now refer to as the 'Tories', would have rejected that label, preferring the term Independent Whig, or even 'Friends of Pitt' in homage to William Pitt after his death. Part of their *raison d'être* revolved around their opposition to their antithesis, the 'Whigs'. As Patricia Ingham has noted in her book *The Brontës*, it was this constant tug of war between the political factions that fascinated the Brontë children, and fuelled the conflicts of their Angrian and Gondal sagas.[3]

Traditionally, Whigs were against absolute monarchy and played a key role in the Glorious Revolution of 1688, when the Protestant William of Orange usurped the throne of the Catholic King James II of England. Whig opposition to supreme royal power positioned them as the more liberal group, as they advocated for full parliamentary control of government. When

A satirical cartoon on the state of William Pitt's Britain, 1804.

McConnel and Kennedy Mills, Manchester:
owned by nouveau riche industrialists.

in power, the Whigs often drove through constitutional reform, such as the Great Reform Act of 1832. By current standards, however, this Act was less than great. It only offered middle-class men the capacity to vote. And it actively banned women from that privilege. Even Chartism, the working-class rights movement of the 1830s and '40s, did not include women in its cry for universal suffrage.

The Tories, on the other hand, were even less liberal than their parliamentary counterparts. According to Samuel Johnson – himself a staunch Tory supporter – a Tory was some-one 'who adheres to the ancient constitution of the state, and the apostolical hierarchy of the Church of England, opposed to a Whig'.[4] The Tories were therefore characterised by their firm following of the establishment and the status quo; they favoured the ancient landowning families, as opposed to the nouveau riche (industrial types). After the French Revolution, the Tories sought to repress any sign of public dissatisfaction, propelled by the fear of an English revolution flaring up in imitation of France's own uprising. They did not seek to represent the people.

Luddites breaking up machinery.

This zero-tolerance approach suited Charlotte's father, Patrick. He witnessed the devastation caused by the Irish rebellion of 1798 and, during his time as the Hartshead-cum-Clifton curate in the West Riding, saw the destruction of the Luddite uprisings, when textile workers protested against the introduction of new technologies. As a consequence, he was fiercely opposed to revolution – and, by extension, major political reform and upheaval. Although he worked hard to fight inequality by introducing educational initiatives and pushing for better sanitary conditions in Haworth, he did so within the pre-existing system.

But Patrick's dual subscriptions to the *Leeds Intelligencer* and *Leeds Mercury* do prove his readiness to engage with the opposing view. In fact, he wrote more frequently to the *Leeds Mercury* than to its political counterpart. He had an abstemious temperament and an acute aversion to revolution – but he was still in many ways a liberal man, largely due to his unconventional past.

At the age of sixteen, he founded his own public school. During his formative years, he held three apprenticeships as a weaver, a blacksmith and a linen draper. He was most likely self-taught and, later in his life, he went on to become a published author and poet. And, at twenty-five, he left his family farm in Ireland for Cambridge University, where he changed his name from Brunty to Brontë. 'Bronte' means 'thunder' in Greek, a fitting name for the authors of *Jane Eyre* and *Wuthering Heights* with their storm-splitting trees and the constant rumblings of violence. As we know, Patrick went on to become perpetual curate of Haworth parsonage. Once he took up this position, he never returned to his homeland.

Politically a Tory, like her father, Charlotte did not align herself with the radicals. One of Charlotte's school-friends, Mary Taylor, wrote to Elizabeth Gaskell after Charlotte's death about her friend's early passion for politics:

> We used to be furious politicians, as one could hardly help being in 1832. She knew the names of the two ministries; the one that resigned, and the one that succeeded and passed the Reform Bill. She worshipped the Duke of Wellington, but said that Sir Robert Peel was not to be trusted; he did not act from principle like the rest, but from expediency. I, being of the furious radical party, told her 'how could any of them trust one another; they were all of them rascals!' Then she would launch out into praises of the Duke of Wellington, referring to his actions; which I could not contradict, as I knew nothing about him. She said she had taken interest in politics ever since she was five years old. She did not get her opinions from her father—that is, not directly—but from the papers, &c., he preferred.[5]

As a young woman, Charlotte was an ardent traditionalist. Her views were in fact more hard-line than those of her father's – as Mary notes, Charlotte was not a mere parrot of Patrick's opinions. She held her own in debates and amazed her friends with knowledge far beyond that of a normal sixteen-year-old. Like Jane Eyre, she had a firm understanding of her own moral compass, even if those morals were based on reactionary views.

Yet Charlotte had little desire to address social issues in her writing. She even wanted other authors, such as William Thackeray and Harriet Martineau, to avoid the inclusion of current affairs in their work, believing that its presence undermined a book's universality and longevity. After all, this was the woman who told the Poet Laureate, Robert Southey, that she wished to be 'for ever known' (see Chapter One). Writing a novel or a poem too focused on contemporary concerns would not lead to fame beyond death.

Charlotte wrote to her publisher that she wished Thackeray 'could be told not to care much for dwelling on the political or religious intrigues of the times'. She added, rather presumptuously, that he 'does not value political or religious intrigue of any age or date'.[6] Her response to Thackeray's literary foray into current affairs tells us more about Charlotte's political apathy than his novel *The History of Henry Esmond*. Over time, Charlotte became less and less engaged with politics. In her letter to Gaskell, Mary Taylor uses the past tense: 'we *used* to be furious politicians.'

Her more trenchant beliefs mellowed – at least, her declaration of those beliefs did. Notably, she remarked that her enthusiasm with all things military – one of her first loves – was dampened by experience. On 31 March 1848, still in the early days of *Jane Eyre*'s success, Charlotte wrote to her lifelong friend and the headmistress of Roe Head School, Margaret Wooler, about her changing relationship with war:

I remember well wishing my lot had been cast in the troubled times of the late war, and seeing in its 'exciting' incidents a kind of stimulating charm which it made my pulses beat fast only to think of [...] I have now outlived youth; and, though I dare not say that I have outlived all its illusions – that the romance is quite gone from Life, the veil fallen from Truth, and that I see both in naked reality – yet certainly many things are not to me what they were ten years ago; and amongst the rest, 'the pomp and circumstance of war' have quite lost in my eyes their factitious glitter.[7]

There is an almost audible poignancy in these words. She charts the sobering development of her thoughts towards an end of innocence. As a child, hearing about the Luddite uprisings from her father and revelling in the legacy of the French Revolution, Charlotte had embraced the violent side of life, but not necessarily its reality. War was a shimmering, tantalising otherworld of which she could only dream. Thoughts of battle

Harriet Martineau and William Makepeace Thackeray.

took her beyond her immediate situation and placed her in a realm where being a woman did not matter. In this world, she was free to play-fight and to be a soldier, while also creating her ideal Byronic love interest.

Fast forward ten or so years, and Charlotte had gained an awareness of suffering that led to her disillusionment with conflict. Even the petty parliamentary infighting that had consumed her in her youth became a source of indifference. In a letter to William Smith Williams, her publisher, dated 20 April 1848, she responds to his comments on the Chartists and the government's decision to ignore their demands for more rights. Charlotte agrees with Williams that such neglect is absurd and damages any possibility of 'mutual kindliness':

> I seem to see this fact plainly, though politics are not my study; and though political partisanship is what I would ever wish to avoid as much as religious bigotry; both errors seeming to me fatal to fair views of mankind in general, and just estimate of individual character.[8]

Here, Charlotte states her political stance clearly. No longer a nominal Tory (at least, not openly), she prefers to take up a position based on what she considers to be right and kind. By the middle of 1849, having lost Branwell, Emily and Anne in quick succession, she had become even more disenchanted with the political system. Charlotte's main focus was then on the less tangible, but less changeable forces. In this sense, it seemed that tolerance and objectivity formed the brightest threads of her political philosophy.

A sanitised interior view of a cotton mill.

Class War and Shirley

Despite Charlotte's protestations of her non-partisanship, several critics have identified the political (and deeply biased) subtext of her second published novel, *Shirley*, which is set during the period of industrial depression and Luddite uprisings in the early 1800s. This book is often placed within the 'condition of England' genre of 19th-century literature, dedicated to addressing cultural concerns of the time. *Shirley* was not as well received as *Jane Eyre*, and does not possess the kind of cultural currency that her first novel still enjoys. But it was a departure for Charlotte, an example of her desire to surprise people and defy expectation.

As Terry Eagleton, Philip Rogers and Lucasta Miller have identified, the book was also in fact deeply partisan.[9] Contrary to her comments to W.S. Williams in 1848, Charlotte was not sympathetic to Chartism. Her father's deep hatred of revolution had influenced her own ideas about rioting. That is not to say that, had she been alive today, she would have supported the use of water cannon. But she was not on the side of the underdog.

A Chartist riot.

In his seminal Marxist work on the Brontës, *Myths of Power*, Terry Eagleton identified the link between Charlotte's treatment of the Luddite uprisings and the Chartist movement of the 1830s and 40s. Charlotte backdates her story in order to explore current issues from a safe distance, while also allowing contemporary readers to tune into the subtext. Any reader in 1849 would be keenly aware of the political environment, coming so close after the re-emergence and subsequent defeat of Chartism in 1848 (the events to which Charlotte was referring in her letter to Williams). By addressing famous past riots – which were also about inequality and marginalisation – Charlotte was indirectly commenting on more recent revolts.

This connection places a rather large question mark over Charlotte's liberal credentials, which are attributed primarily because of her proto-feminism. *Shirley* renders the working-class characters practically voiceless and paints them all as two-dimensional, while the reader is encouraged to root for the manufacturers, the aristocracy and the Church – in effect, the establishment and the businessmen.

Moore had expected this attack for days, perhaps weeks; he was prepared for it at every point. He had fortified and garrisoned his mill, which in itself was a strong building. He was a cool, brave man; he stood to the defence with unflinching firmness. Those who were with him caught his spirit, and copied his demeanour. The rioters had never been so met before. At other mills they had attacked they had found no resistance; an organized, resolute defence was what they never dreamed of encountering. When their leaders saw the steady fire kept up from the mill, witnessed the composure and determination of its owner, heard themselves coolly defied and invited on to death, and beheld their men falling wounded round them, they felt that nothing was to be done here. In haste they mustered their forces, drew them away from the building. A roll was called over, in which the men answered to figures instead of names. They dispersed wide over the fields, leaving silence and ruin behind them. The attack, from its commencement to its termination, had not occupied an hour […]

It was no cheering spectacle. These premises were now a mere blot of desolation on the fresh front of the summer dawn. All the copse up the Hollow was shady and dewy, the hill at its head was green; but just here, in the centre of the sweet glen, Discord, broken loose in the night from control, had beaten the ground with his stamping hoofs, and left it waste and pulverized. The mill yawned all ruinous with unglazed frames; the yard was thickly bestrewn with stones and brickbats; and close under the mill, with the glittering fragments of the shattered windows, muskets and other weapons lay here and there. More than one deep crimson stain

was visible on the gravel, a human body lay quiet on
its face near the gates, and five or six wounded men
writhed and moaned in the bloody dust.[10]

There is no mention of what is at stake in the conflict.
The fact that families were starving (not only because of the
introduction of new machines, but because of the knock-
on impact of the French Revolution on trade) is nowhere to
be seen in Charlotte's description of the battle. Instead, and
rather characteristically, she focuses on the blood and desolation, and – again perhaps predictably – on Robert Moore,
the mill owner. Charlotte returns to war and violence, but
instead of offering a glimpse into the lived devastation of
battle's aftermath, she gives us the ruined mill and a name-
less 'human body' lying in the gravel.

Unlike in Elizabeth Gaskell's *North and South*, in which
we are invited into the homes of the striking mill workers,
Shirley offers us a one-sided perspective. We see Moore's
war preparations, his battle-hardiness. Just like the Duke
of Wellington, that grand 'demigod', Moore is described in
heroic terms. And where are the rioters, the workers? They
are merely a faceless mob, left writhing and moaning in the
wake of Moore's superior forces. Despite her best efforts to
renounce partisanship, Charlotte's 'condition of England'
novel picks a side – and it is not necessarily the one with
which modern audiences would agree.

A Victorian governess.

THE WOMAN QUESTION

Was Charlotte a Proto-Feminist?

The 'Woman Question' was one of the major issues of the 19th century. It centred around the social position of women, their legal and economic status in particular. Until 1882, when the Married Women's Property Act came into effect, married women were invisible in legal terms. Upon marriage, a woman's property, wealth and identity were subsumed into that of her husband. She became non-existent. Throughout the mid-1800s, however, there was a backlash against such suppression, and this was born out in the debates surrounding the Woman Question.

As mentioned in Chapter One, Charlotte was acutely aware of her need to earn money. Her father was not a wealthy man and, despite a small inheritance from her Aunt Branwell, it was desirable for Charlotte and her sisters to find their own income. Emily hated her job as a governess, lasting only six months. Charlotte and Anne stuck it out for a bit longer, but Charlotte's real ambition was to become a published writer. After

*Frontispiece of an 18th-century cookery book by Hannah Glasse,
one of a small number of women to be published at that time.*

discovering a stash of Emily's poems, she began considering the
world of writing as a financial alternative. In 1846, a publisher,
Aylott and Jones, produced a collection of the sisters' poetry
under the infamous pseudonyms Currer, Ellis and Acton Bell.
They had to pay for the printing and binding themselves, and the
poems received minimal attention and only sold two copies. But
the reviews the collection did acquire were favourable. And this
first taste of a literary life emboldened all three in their pursuit of
success – *Jane Eyre*, of course, was published the following year.

For three young women to seek publication at this time, to
essentially step outside of their domestic sphere into the public
eye, was no mean feat. The fact that they disguised their female
names proves the prejudice levelled at women writers. Even the
phrase 'women writers' lingers into today's literary lexicon – as
though women write about specifically feminine things, while
men write about everything else.

In her early twenties, Charlotte sought the advice of the Poet
Laureate, Robert Southey. His letter, and the stand-out remark
that literature 'cannot be the business of a woman's life, and it
ought not to be', is a recurring point of discussion in Brontë biographies. Taken within the context of his letter, the sentence feels
less vindictive and more paternal – but it is no less patronising:

[…] It is not my advice that you have asked as to the direction of your talents, but my opinion of them; and yet the opinion may be worth little, and the advice much. You evidently possess, and in no inconsiderable degree, what Wordsworth calls 'the faculty of verse'. I am not depreciating it when I say that in these times it is not rare. Many volumes of poems are now published every year without attracting public attention, any one of which, if it had appeared half a century ago, would have obtained a high reputation for its author. Whoever, therefore, is ambitious of distinction in this way, ought to be prepared for disappointment.

But it is not with a view to distinction that you should cultivate this talent, if you consult your own happiness. I, who have made literature my profession, and devoted my life to it, and have never for a moment repented of the deliberate choice, think myself nevertheless bound in duty to caution every young man who applies as an aspirant to me for encouragement and advice against taking so perilous a course. You will say, that a woman has no need of such a caution: there can be no peril in it for her. In a certain sense this is true; but there is a danger of which I would, with all kindness and all earnestness, warn you. The day dreams in which you habitually indulge are likely to induce a distempered state of mind; and in proportion as all the ordinary uses of the world seem to you flat and unprofitable, you will be unfitted for them without becoming fitted for anything else. Literature cannot be the business of a woman's life, and it ought not to be. The more she is engaged in her proper duties, the less leisure will she have for it even as an accomplishment and a recreation. To those duties you have not yet been called, and, when you are, you will be less eager for celebrity. You will not seek in imagination for excitement, of which the vicissitudes of this life, and the anxieties from which you must not hope to be exempted, be your state what it may, will bring with them but too much [...][11]

Southey makes allusions to hysteria – the possibility of Charlotte's 'day dreams' inducing a 'distempered state of mind'. Literature was often characterised as having the power to turn a woman's mind. Consider Jane Austen's *Northanger Abbey*, in which its heroine Catherine Morland fantasises about duels and Byronic heroes as a result of her bedtime reading, namely Ann Radcliffe's *The Mysteries of Udolpho*. Here, Southey is attempting to steer Charlotte towards a more mundane and 'normal' way of living. He tells her that her life will undoubtedly and inevitably be dull, far less exciting than any story or book. She must exercise due temperance in order to avoid disappointment or, worse, madness.

A scene from The Woman in White. Wilkie Collins's novels challenged traditional women's roles in literature, doubtless influenced by the Brontës.

Shirley has often been deemed a proto-feminist novel, specifically because its female characters are outspoken in their domestic dissatisfaction. Shirley – the title character of the book – is a landowning heiress who knows how to shoot a gun. She is called 'Captain Keeldar' even by conservative/traditional male characters, proving her tendency to slip into the role of gentleman on occasion. In fact, her parents named her 'Shirley' – typically a boy's name in the 19th century – when they discovered that their first-born child was, disappointingly, a girl. This led to the popularisation of 'Shirley' as a woman's name. Her role as both rich young woman and battle-ready captain means that she is often found raging against the establishment, usually the men at its helm:

> 'Men, I believe, fancy women's minds something like those of children. Now that is a mistake […] If men could see us as we really are, they would be a little amazed; but the cleverest, the acutest men are often under an illusion about women: they do not read them in a true light: they misapprehend them, both for good and evil; their good woman is a queer thing, half doll, half angel; their bad woman almost always a fiend.'[12]

Even the 'cleverest, the acutest' men fail to comprehend the intellectual capacity of women. Or, perhaps, it is especially this kind of man who prefers his woman submissive and silent. Yet even the gender-fluid Shirley ends the novel in a predictable way. She marries Louis Moore, the well-educated and sardonic tutor of her cousin. There is nothing wrong with a happy ending. But it is, in a sense, disappointing that Shirley's rowdiness and anger is dissipated by the novel's ending. Even less appealing is the fact that her inherited wealth and power becomes the possession of Louis. He is made magistrate, while she is admired for wearing grand outfits.

Women workers in a Manchester cotton mill.

The novel's other female protagonist, Caroline, is also an advocate for changing the role of women, specifically in relation to work:

'Nobody,' she went on — 'nobody in particular is to blame, that I can see, for the state in which things are; and I cannot tell, however much I puzzle over it, how they are to be altered for the better; but I feel there is something wrong somewhere. I believe single women should have more to do—better chances of interesting and profitable occupation than they possess now. And when I speak thus I have no impression that I displease God by my words; that I am either impious or impatient, irreligious or sacrilegious. My consolation is, indeed, that God hears many a groan, and compassionates much grief which man stops his ears against, or frowns on with impotent contempt. I say *impotent*, for I observe that to such grievances as society cannot readily cure it usually forbids utterance, on pain of its scorn, this scorn being only a sort of tinselled cloak to its deformed weakness. People hate to be reminded of ills they are unable or unwilling to remedy. Such reminder, in forcing on them a sense of their own incapacity, or a more painful sense of an obligation to make some unpleasant effort, troubles their ease and shakes their self-complacency. Old maids, like the houseless and unemployed poor, should not ask for a place and an occupation in the world; the demand disturbs the happy and rich—it disturbs parents. Look at the numerous families of girls in this neighbourhood—the Armitages, the Birtwhistles, the Sykeses. The brothers of these girls are every one in business or in professions; they have something to do. Their sisters have no earthly employment but household work and sewing, no earthly pleasure but an unprofitable visiting, and no hope, in all their life to come, of anything better. This stagnant state of things makes them decline in health. They are never well, and their minds and views shrink to wondrous narrowness. The great wish, the sole aim of every one of them is to be married, but the majority will never marry; they will die as they now live. They scheme, they plot, they dress to ensnare husbands. The gentlemen turn them into ridicule; they don't want them; they hold them very cheap. They say—I have heard them say it with sneering laughs many a time—the matrimonial market is overstocked. Fathers say so likewise, and are angry with their daughters when they observe their manoeuvres—they order them to stay at home. What do they expect them to do at home? If you ask, they would answer, sew and cook. They expect them to do this, and this only, contentedly, regularly, uncomplainingly, all their lives long, as if they had no germs of faculties for anything else—a doctrine as reasonable to hold as it would be that the fathers have no faculties but for eating what their daughters cook or for wearing what they sew. Could men live so themselves? Would they not be very weary? And when there came no relief to their weariness, but only reproaches at its slightest manifestation, would not their weariness ferment in time to frenzy? Lucretia, spinning at midnight in the midst of her maidens, and Solomon's virtuous woman are often quoted as patterns of what 'the sex,' as they say, ought to be. I don't know. Lucretia, I dare say, was a most worthy sort of person, much like my cousin Hortense Moore; but she kept her servants up very late. I should not have liked to be amongst the number of the maidens. Hortense would just work me and Sarah in that fashion, if she could, and neither of us would bear it. The 'virtuous woman,' again, had her household up in the very middle of the night; she 'got breakfast over,' as Mrs. Sykes says, before one o'clock a.m.; but *she* had something more to do than spin and give out portions. She was a manufacturer—she made fine linen and sold it; she was an agriculturist—she bought estates and planted vineyards. *That* woman was a manager. She was what the matrons hereabouts call 'a clever woman.' On the whole, I like her a good deal better than Lucretia; but I don't believe either Mr. Armitage or Mr. Sykes could have got the advantage of her in a bargain. Yet I like her. 'Strength and honour were her clothing; the heart of her husband safely trusted in her. She opened her mouth with wisdom; in her tongue was the law of kindness; her children rose up and called her blessed; her husband also praised her.' King of Israel! your model of a woman is a worthy model! But are we, in these days, brought up to be like her? Men of Yorkshire! do your daughters reach this royal standard? Can they reach it? Can you help them to reach it? Can you give them a field in which their faculties may be exercised and grow? Men of England! look at your poor girls, many of them fading around you, dropping off in consumption or decline; or, what is worse, degenerating to sour old maids—envious, back-biting, wretched, because life is a desert to them; or, what is worst of all, reduced to strive, by scarce modest coquetry and debasing artifice, to gain that position and consideration by marriage which to celibacy is denied. Fathers! cannot you alter these things? Perhaps not all at once; but consider the matter well when it is brought before you, receive it as a theme worthy of thought; do not dismiss it with an idle jest or an unmanly insult. You would wish to be proud of your daughters, and not to blush for them; then seek for them an interest and an occupation which shall raise them above the flirt, the manoeuvrer, the mischief-making tale-bearer. Keep your girls' minds narrow and fettered; they will still be a plague and a care, sometimes a disgrace to you. Cultivate them—give them scope and work; they will be your gayest companions in health, your tenderest nurses in sickness, your most faithful prop in age.'[13]

Caroline ends this rousing internal monologue with the view that 'men of England' should educate their daughters and wom-enfolk for their own benefit. For bourgeois women like Caroline and Shirley, then, the real Woman Question revolved around their idleness, their lack of purpose in life other than mar-riage and babies. There were few opportunities for middle- and

A draper's shop: respectable employment for a woman.

upper-class women to find work. The option of becoming a governess, a position which the three Brontë sisters found unappealing but necessary, was often the only one available to more genteel women. That is, if you were unwilling to look beyond the status quo. But, even if a woman wanted to get a job (as Caroline repeatedly expresses an interest in), they had to contend with the social prejudices associated with (certain) women working.

Working-class women were, of course, already working; so, Caroline's distress is plainly a class issue. It reminds me of Emma Thompson's speech when she won an Oscar for her screenplay of *Sense and Sensibility*. She thanked Sydney Pollack for asking all the right questions: 'like, why couldn't these women go out and get a job? Why indeed!'[14] It was not necessarily that women did not wish to work – the social structure of their class maintained strict barriers against their mobility and economic status.

Upon reading *Shirley*, and in relation to the class-based problem of working women, Charlotte's long-time friend Mary Taylor was less than impressed with the novel's treatment of the Woman Question. On 29 April 1850, she wrote to Charlotte with some choice words on the subject:

> I have seen some extracts from *Shirley* in which you talk
> of women working. And this first duty, this great neces-
> sity you seem to think that *some* women may indulge
> in – if they give up marriage & don't make themselves
> too disagreeable to the other sex. You are a coward and
> a traitor. A woman who works is by that alone better
> than one who does not; and a woman who does not
> happen to be rich and who still earns no money and
> does not wish to do so, is guilty of a great fault, almost
> a crime [...][15]

Having emigrated to New Zealand in 1842, and consequently opened up a draper's shop with her female cousin,
Mary Taylor was far more radical and daring than Charlotte.
For Mary, the Woman Question was a deeply class-based
economic issue and one she felt other women had a duty to
confront. The actions of all women mattered. Charlotte was
not bold enough for Mary. Despite being a published author
purely through her own initiative, Charlotte's proto-feminism still fell short. Perhaps it fell short *because* she was a
successful author. After *Jane Eyre*, she had a platform from
which she could promote her own proto-feminist agenda.
From Mary's perspective, Charlotte failed to utilise this stage
effectively.

Charlotte was not, then, a perfect proto-feminist by any
means. She approached topics like the Woman Question from
the position of her educated privilege and traditionalist politics. Yet the very fact that she broke away – for however short
a period – from her domestic duties and imagined an alternative career for herself shows her willingness to think beyond
her situation. She was, and remains, a moderate but by no
means marginal revolutionary.

A caricature exemplifying racist colonial attitudes in Jamaica.

Was Jane Eyre a Feminist?

The character of Jane Eyre is undoubtedly independent and brave and she speaks her mind in the face of injustice. But her reputation as a feminist does also come with some caveats.

Yes, she *is* fierce and feisty, and she has aspirations. In life, she is always looking towards the horizon. Never does she allow her status as an orphan with no money and few prospects deter her from gaining employment and an identity. As a woman in an inherently patriarchal society, without the vote and without legal rights, Jane has to assert herself or no one else will. She has no financial support, no home, no friends, no family, no connections to speak of. All she owns is her mind and her body. From this, she builds the life she wants.

In this sense, I think Jane *is* a feminist – or, at least, a proto-feminist. But part of her journey relies on the marginalisation of others in order for her to succeed. The book is an expression of individualism. Throughout, we see events through Jane's 'I' and eyes. In order to triumph in life, she must overcome the injustices and immorality of others. She has to place her identity in opposition to these obstacles, effectively destroying them and then emerging victorious.

One clear example of the importance of overcoming the 'Other' in *Jane Eyre* is the description of Bertha Mason. In order for Jane to marry Rochester, Bertha – 'the mad woman in the attic' and Rochester's legal wife – must die. The allegedly promiscuous Creole woman must be sacrificed for the pure English girl's gain. As we saw in the previous chapter, Bertha is dehumanised: 'What it was, whether beast or human being, one could not, at first sight, tell: it groveled, seemingly, on all fours; it snatched and growled like some strange wild animal.'[16] She is not fully a human being, but a savage 'it' in civilised clothes.

The ambiguity surrounding Bertha's racial identity enhances her Otherness. As the daughter of a white colonial, Bertha sits in the liminal space between 'civilised' and 'Other': she is neither English nor Jamaican; as a Creole, she is both. Slavery had only recently been abolished in 1833 when Charlotte wrote the novel, and the spectres of colonialism and racism hover over Bertha's presence at Thornfield. Rochester attempts to justify the depiction of Bertha as subhuman by providing her with a heritage of madness, one based on immoral behaviour and racial profiling:

> Bertha Mason is mad; and she came of a mad family; idiots and maniacs through three generations! Her mother, the Creole, was both a madwoman and a drunkard! —as I found out after I had wed the daughter: for they were silent on family secrets before. Bertha, like a dutiful child, copied her parent in both points.[17]

Rochester aligns her mother's Creole identity with that of insanity and drunkenness. As a woman from another country, and from Rochester's male aristocratic perspective, Bertha embodies everything that is impure and uncivilised in the world – with Jane as her physical opposite.

'Mad' Bertha.

Notably, Jane admonishes Rochester for his cruel, dismissive view of Bertha. After all, 'she cannot help being mad'.[18] Yet we cannot forget that the story is told from the perspective of a much older Jane. She may have felt sympathy for Bertha's situation, but is still guilty of automatically associating Rochester's wife with a 'hyena' instead of a human being. It is Jane, not Rochester, who calls Bertha 'it'.

Through 21st-century eyes, the dehumanisation of Bertha is not feminist. As Chimamanda Ngozi Adichie pointed out in her ground-shifting 'We Should All Be Feminists' speech in 2013, the definition of a feminist is 'a person who believes in the social, political, and economic equality of the sexes'.[19] (The speech received Beyoncé's seal of approval when she included a sound-bite of Adichie in her 2014 song '***Flawless'.[20]) On every level, Bertha is not considered an equal. Through the laws of marriage, Rochester possesses her wealth. Politically, she is marginalised both as a woman, as a person with a mental illness, and as a Creole Jamaican. And, hidden away in the attic room, she is a social pariah with only the gin-loving Grace Poole for company.

So, even if we want to maintain Charlotte's image as a liberal-minded feminist writer, we cannot and should not dismiss Bertha as simply a colonial metaphor. Nor can we continue to consider her as a psychological representative of Jane's darker, more passionate side. As Jean Rhys' seminal novel *Wide Sargasso Sea* proves, Bertha (or, as Rhys renames her, Antoinette Cosway) can be resurrected and redefined as a woman with a history, a name, a home and a mind all of her own. Just as Jane has.

This doesn't necessarily have to negate Jane's proto-feminism. It is particularly unfair to blame Jane for the fate of Bertha. By doing so, we are excusing Rochester's role. After all, he is the one who incarcerates his wife and almost succeeds in committing bigamy. He may claim that he locks Bertha away for her own safety and for the safety of others – a point perhaps proven by her attack on her brother and her intimidation of Jane. Yet there is a lingering selfishness surrounding Rochester's actions. While his mad wife languishes on the third floor of Thornfield, Rochester is busy gallivanting around Europe, seducing women and spending Bertha's money.

The novel's approach to sex, however, has helped to earn it its place as a proto-feminist text. Many researchers and readers have noted the sadomasochism running through Jane's narrative, particularly in her relationship with Rochester.[21] Elaine Showalter has even interpreted the red room scene (see Chapter Four) in terms of Victorian flagellation pornography.[22] So, there's little doubt Charlotte can beat *Fifty Shades of Grey* at its own game – red room, and all. It's also worth bearing in mind that Charlotte herself enjoyed calling Monsieur Heger her 'master', and that *The Professor* is also infused with an undercurrent

'O! So masterful, and she so weak…!'

of violence based on this teacher/pupil exchange.[23] Charlotte didn't need the elaborate descriptions or explicit dialogue to challenge, and in many cases offend, contemporary views of sex. Simply by expressing the intense connection between Jane and Rochester, she was pushing boundaries.

When Jane and Rochester are finally engaged, he is constantly trying to assert his dominance by buying her vibrant dresses and beautiful jewellery, all of which she rejects (except the bridal veil, which Bertha later destroys). At one point, Rochester's smile resembles that of a sultan bestowing a smirk on a slave.[24] The image is unsettling, especially when you consider it in light of his treatment of Bertha. Yet the novel was more progressive in its representation of female sexuality, and this was one of the reasons why reviewers reacted so strongly against aspects of the novel. One reviewer likened Jane and Rochester's courtship to that of 'kangaroos' due to its 'animal appetite'.[25] For 1847, it was radical for a writer, let alone a woman, to describe the 'fervent, solemn passion' that kindles 'in pure, powerful flame' and 'fuses' Jane and Rochester.[26] But Jane also resists Rochester's controlling ways – she can be forceful and combative. She was not willing to be a slave to his sultan. This resistance against female submissiveness was provocative and daring. Charlotte was placing a woman's needs at the centre of her novel and this included her sexuality.

Yet it is ultimately Jane's powerful voice – not her passionate interactions with Rochester – that sustains the reader throughout her 'autobiography', as well as her striving for independence, for meaning, and for an identity she can accept and love. She is also acutely aware of the injustices levelled at women:

Bertha destroys Jane's veil.

It is in vain to say human beings ought to be satisfied with tranquillity: they must have action; and they will make it if they cannot find it. Millions are condemned to a stiller doom than mine, and millions are in silent revolt against their lot. Nobody knows how many rebellions besides political rebellions ferment in the masses of life which people earth. Women are supposed to be very calm generally: but women feel just as men feel; they need exercise for their faculties, and a field for their efforts, as much as their brothers do; they suffer from too rigid a restraint, too absolute a stagnation, precisely as men would suffer; and it is narrow-minded in their more privileged fellow-creatures to say that they ought to confine themselves to making puddings and knitting stockings, to playing on the piano and embroidering bags. It is thoughtless to condemn them, or laugh at them, if they seek to do more or learn more than custom has pronounced necessary for their sex.[27]

Charlotte, Anne and Emily all had domestic duties to attend to in the parsonage, including pudding-making and embroidery. Although the above words come from the mind of Jane Eyre, I can imagine Charlotte mouthing them to herself, eyes closed in concentration. It is a sudden breaking up of and breaking into the narrative, an interjection that the author clearly wished the narrator, Jane, to express fervently. While it is not always appropriate to align the narrative voice with that of the author, in this instance (and in *Shirley*) it is difficult to believe that Charlotte's own thoughts on the subject were far from Jane's. We see this kind of interjection throughout the novel. Again and again, despite her small stature and status, Jane avows her equality with – and sometimes even her superiority over – powerful men and women. In one of the most famous – and, in my mind, stirring – expressions of selfhood in British fiction, Jane confronts Rochester when she believes he will soon marry the snobbish Blanche Ingram, leaving her alone once more:

> 'Do you think I can stay to become nothing to you? Do you think I am an automaton? —a machine without feelings? and can bear to have my morsel of bread snatched from my lips, and my drop of living water dashed from my cup? Do you think, because I am poor, obscure, plain, and little, I am soulless and heartless? You think wrong! —I have as much soul as you, —and full as much heart! And if God had gifted me with some beauty and much wealth, I should have made it as hard for you to leave me, as it is now for me to leave you. I am not talking to you now through the medium of custom, conventionalities, nor even of mortal flesh; —it is my spirit that addresses your spirit; just as if both had passed through the grave, and we stood at God's feet, equal, —as we are!'[28]

Who could help but feel an instant connection with these words? A few lines later she breaks out again in one of the most resonating and memorable phrases in English literature:

> 'I am no bird and no net ensnares me; I am a free human being with an independent will.'[29]

These words do not erase the complexity and contradictions of Jane's relationship to proto-feminism. But it is here, in this declaration of self, in which Jane Eyre's basic humanity lies.

SIX

(DESPERATELY)
SEEKING
CHARLOTTE

Although a lot has changed in the last 200 years, you can still find traces of Charlotte in most of the places she visited. If you go to the Brontë Parsonage Museum, run by the Brontë Society, then you will be climbing the same stairs that the Brontë family walked up and down for more than fifty years. Conservation and replication are now the standard approaches adopted by museums across Britain, and the Brontë Parsonage is no different. By recreating the living space of the family to become a kind of living museum, the Parsonage Museum brings to life their everyday habits and routines, enabling visitors to imagine more clearly the three sisters circling the table in their living room or kneading bread while reading poetry in the kitchen.

But it is not just the Haworth parsonage: locations with unconfirmed links to the Brontës are bringing history (and fiction) to life, too. Ponden Hall, approximately three miles from Haworth, is one of these places. Its association with the Brontës – primarily Branwell and Emily, who reportedly spent many afternoons in the house's well-stocked library – is largely based on conjecture and hearsay. No letter or fragment confirms

Ponden Hall, in an image from 1900.

Ponden Hall as a principal influence on *Wuthering Heights*. Only Patrick Brontë's sermon and letter to the *Leeds Mercury* about the Crow Hill Bog Burst in 1824 provide an account of his four youngest children (Charlotte, Branwell, Emily and Anne) visiting Ponden Hall as a place of shelter during the mudslide and thunderstorm. In both his sermon and his letter, Patrick likened the bog burst to an earthquake and suggested that it was a warning sign from God imploring sinners to change their ways.

Although we don't truly know the extent of the Brontë connection with Ponden Hall, it is still very much a go-to destination for Brontë hunters. And why not? All of the little speculative stories surrounding the family, including the more sensational ones in Gaskell's *The Life of Charlotte Brontë*, add something to our impression and understanding of them. It shows our ongoing desire to find connections in unlikely and unconfirmed places, and to fill in the gaps wherever we can through locations and architecture.

These days, Ponden Hall is a lovely B&B with a room named after the Earnshaw family in *Wuthering Heights* with a replica of the box-bed in which Heathcliff dies and where Lockwood encounters Cathy's ghost through the window. Depending on your perspective, this is either an uncanny or exciting way to spend an evening. This level of restoration – and, in this case, recreation – allows visitors to immerse themselves in the world of the Brontës, placing tourists in a strange in-between space where they are neither in the present nor the past, in fiction nor in fact. It is like pushing through the fourth wall and finding yourself in a theatrical set.

Authenticity is one of the hardest aspects to capture for tourists, especially with objects and locations preserved or resurrected from the past. This is because, by their very anachronistic nature, they no longer really belong in the present. Of course, the alternative of providing wordy descriptions and fuzzy photographs is far less engaging than the recreated bedroom of a famous author or the glass display cabinet filled with their best clothes. Even if it ends up being a reproduction, these materials and the places in which they are housed somehow feel closer to that previous reality. As literary and historical tourists, we crave something more personal and intimate, something truer.

Perhaps it was this something I was hoping to find in that graveyard. The photo might look staged and maybe even morbid, but documenting your place in a particular setting, especially when it is historical, is an instinct that people have been acting on for centuries. It is like writing in the margins of a book, spray-painting a wall or carving on a tree 'I woz here', the equivalent of writing 'I am'. Maybe it is too far to say visiting and photographing famous sites are declarations of existence. But – to me, at least – it is a declaration of affinity, a way of stating without words my appreciation of and connection with the Brontës. By taking the time to learn about these locations, we are positioning ourselves in a timeline and, in a small way, we become part of the place's history.

We want to know exactly where Charlotte, Anne, Emily, Branwell and the rest of the family went, what they read and whom they met. And that desire to know more and more often requires imagination and the capacity to suspend disbelief. Pushing the scepticism aside, history often involves a healthy dose of uncertainty and it revolves around the need to discover hidden connections. Does it matter that the box-bed in the 'Earnshaw' room is *not* 'the real thing'? No. Trying to trace the experiences and emotions of the long-dead and famous often hinges on speculation and ambiguity – and that is all part of the fun.

In order to aid your own Brontë-seeking expeditions, here is a selection of famous and not-so-famous places connected to Charlotte and her family. Happy Brontë hunting!

YORKSHIRE

Brontë Parsonage Museum, Haworth

Anyone who wants to learn more about the Brontë family should start here. The Brontë Society acquired the property in 1928, when the Haworth-born wool merchant and lifelong Brontë Society member, Sir James Roberts, bought the parsonage and gave the deeds to the Society. Since then, it has become the hub of all things Brontë – whether you want to see the family's possessions, to read about 19th-century Haworth, or to delve deeper into the siblings' childhood pastimes, this is the museum for you. It is also a fantastic research base, housing the largest Brontë collection in the world. (See illustration on chapter opening page.)

Scarborough

In May 1849, Charlotte and her best friend Ellen Nussey accompanied Anne Brontë to Scarborough, in the hope that the sea air would improve her health. Sadly, it did not. On 28 May 1849, Anne died at the Wood's Lodgings, No.2 The Cliffs. Today, a blue plaque marks the location of these lodgings, where the Grand Hotel now stands. Anne is buried at St Mary's Church on Castle Hill, where you can pay your respects at her original gravestone and the new one laid by the Brontë Society in 2011.

Castle Hill and St Mary's Church, Scarborough (1850s).

Filey seafront, near Cliff House, in the mid-19th century.

Filey

After Anne's death in Scarborough, Charlotte and Ellen moved eight miles down the coast to Filey to recuperate. They stayed at Cliff House on Belle Vue Street, where Charlotte returned in 1852, this time alone, to recover from a bout of ill health and to visit Anne's grave, three years on from her death. Charlotte wrote to Ellen of her decision to go to Filey by herself: 'I am at Filey utterly alone. Do not be angry. The step is right.'[1] Cliff House is now the Bronte Vinery restaurant and features a special plaque to commemorate Charlotte's stay.

Thornton

Although the Brontës are most often associated with Haworth, none of the children was born there. Charlotte, Anne, Emily and Branwell were all born in a terraced house on Market Street in the village of Thornton. Situated on the outskirts of Bradford, not far from Haworth, the siblings (except Anne, the baby) spent the first few years of their lives here. In 1820, Patrick left his role as curate at the Old Bell Chapel and the family moved to Haworth. Their house in Thornton is now an Italian café and delicatessen, named after Emily Brontë.

Norton Conyers, Ripon

Charlotte visited Norton Conyers in 1839, where she heard the legend of a mad woman living in a remote attic chamber in the house, a room still known as 'Mad Mary's Room'. The similarity between this myth and Bertha Mason's situation in *Jane Eyre* has positioned the house as a primary influence for Rochester's Thornfield Hall. Its inspiration was confirmed in 2004 when, during major renovations, a blocked staircase leading to the attic rooms was discovered. You can visit the recently restored Norton Conyers today and see the resemblance for yourself.

Ponden Hall

Although the connection between the Brontë family and Ponden Hall has been well documented, it has never been confirmed. It's still a fascinating place to visit, though. Now a B&B, the house once boasted one of the largest private libraries in the West Riding and even housed a Shakespeare First Folio. If Emily and Branwell did regularly visit Ponden Hall, there's little doubt the library would have been their favourite room. The property was originally built in 1634 for the Heaton family, but the main building was rebuilt in 1801 – the year *Wuthering Heights* begins. For the full Brontë experience at Ponden Hall, you can book the 'Earnshaw' room, with its *Wuthering Heights* box-bed. And if sleeping in a wooden box-bed is not your thing, you can always have some tea and take a tour.

Salts Mill, Saltaire, near Bradford.

Salts Mill, Saltaire

The vast Salts Mill and model village of Saltaire was built by Sir Titus Salt in 1853 and, after he and then his son died, it was saved from bankruptcy and taken over by Sir James Roberts – the same Haworth man who bought the Brontë Haworth Parsonage and bequeathed it to the nation. Today, Saltaire is a UNESCO World Heritage Site and a cultural haven. Salts Mill has not only exhibitions on the history of Saltaire and the Mill, but also a permanent exhibition of David Hockney's work. There's lots of interesting shopping, too: for books, art supplies, musical instruments, antiques, jewellery and textiles, along with a restaurant serving tasty food – definitely worth a day trip.

Red House, Gomersal

Red House was the home of Mary Taylor, one of Charlotte's best friends whom she met at Roe Head School. Her family were wool merchants, but they were not necessarily wealthy – when he died, Mary's father left significant debts, leading her to emigrate to New Zealand. It was in this Grade II* listed building, however, that Charlotte and her friend had their heated political debates. It was also the inspiration behind Briarmains, the home of the lively Yorke family in *Shirley*: 'But if Briar-chapel seemed alive, so also did Briarmains: though certainly the mansion appeared to enjoy a quieter phase of existence

From an early edition of Shirley.

than the temple; some of its windows too were a-glow'.[2] These beautifully lit stained glass windows can still be seen today at the Red House Museum, where you can have a guided tour and discover more about the house's Brontë links.

WHAT TO READ ON THE WAY

No trip to Brontë Country is complete without reading at least one of the sisters' famous novels: Emily's *Wuthering Heights* (1847), Charlotte's *Jane Eyre* (1847), and Anne's *The Tenant of Wildfell Hall* (1848).

Elizabeth Gaskell's *The Life of Charlotte Brontë* (1857).

Haworth Through Time by Steven Wood (Amberley Publishing, 2009).

LANCASHIRE

Cowan Bridge

Situated not far from Kirkby Lonsdale (indeed, not far from Haworth, and easily visited together), Cowan Bridge was home to the Clergy Daughters' School, which opened in 1824 and provided a cut-price yet still high quality education for daughters of the clergy. Maria and Elizabeth, the two eldest Brontë sisters, arrived in July 1824, followed by Charlotte three weeks later and Emily in November. After less than a year, Maria and Elizabeth were diagnosed with tuberculosis, and subsequently withdrawn from the school. They died within six weeks of each other at the ages of eleven and ten respectively. The school was immortalised as the cruel Lowood School in *Jane Eyre* and Charlotte's older sister Maria is said to be the inspiration for Jane's best friend, Helen Burns. In 1833, the school moved to the healthier area of Casterton. The original building (except the dormitory room, which was destroyed in a fire) is now a row of residential cottages.

The Clergy Daughters' School, Cowan Bridge.

Wycoller Hall, thought to be the model for Ferndean Manor.

Wycoller Hall

Just over the Haworth moors lies the village of Wycoller, which it's believed Charlotte and Emily frequently visited. In fact, Wycoller Hall – a 16th-century manor house – is thought to be the inspiration behind Ferndean Manor, the secluded abode Rochester retreats to after Bertha's death. Much of the house is now a ruin, but it remains a conservation area with an onsite museum about its history. It is also the beginning of the Brontë Way walk, which leads over the moors to Haworth. Sadly, in 2015, Lancashire County Council announced plans to withdraw funding for the property, meaning the management, maintenance and ranger service would be cut. Although there has been a petition canvassing against such action, it is a stark reminder that even Brontë heritage sites can come under threat.

THE LAKE DISTRICT

Briery Close

Charlotte visited Sir James and Lady Kay Shuttleworth at their summer house near Lake Windermere in August 1850. Not only was this Charlotte's first visit to the Lake District; it was also where she met her future biographer and fellow novelist, Elizabeth Gaskell. During the last five years of Charlotte's life, the two women became friends and regular correspondents. Briery Close is now a residential home, altered almost beyond recognition, but the importance of the Lake District, and the Lake Poets, to Charlotte remains intact.

Fox How

During her stay at Briery Close, Charlotte visited the widow and daughters of Dr Thomas Arnold, the well-known headmaster of Rugby School and Regius Professor of History at Oxford, who had died eight years previously. Charlotte greatly admired Dr Arnold's views on the Church, but her visit to Fox How, though pleasant, did not live up to her high expectations – she found Dr Arnold's family to be less intellectual and less warm than hoped. Arnold's son, the poet Matthew Arnold, wrote the elegy 'Haworth Churchyard, April, 1855' after Charlotte's death. It imagines Charlotte and her siblings lying together in Haworth graveyard, a typically romanticised vision that was in fact inaccurate: the sisters and brother were all – except Anne – buried together in Haworth church.

The Knoll, Ambleside

Harriet Martineau, the writer and economist and Charlotte's on-off friend, lived in this once ivy-covered house on the top of Lake Windermere. In mid-December 1850, Charlotte visited Harriet at her home for a week and, during the trip, she

Low Wood Hotel, near Ambleside, on Lake Windermere.

met Matthew Arnold for the first time. His poem, 'Haworth Churchyard, April, 1855', opens 'under Loughrigg', the mountain on the foot of which Harriet's house stands, and proceeds to reminisce about the evening Arnold met Charlotte in the company of Martineau and Wordsworth's son-in-law, Edward Quillinan. He is mistaken when he writes that he witnessed Charlotte and Harriet meeting; they were already friends:

> Where, under Loughrigg, the stream
> Of Rotha sparkles through fields
> Vested for ever with green,
> Four years since, in the house
> Of a gentle spirit, now dead—
> Wordsworth's son-in-law, friend—
> I saw the meeting of two
> Gifted women. The one,
> Brilliant with recent renown,
> Young, unpractised, had told
> With a master's accent her feign'd
> Story of passionate life;

The other, mature in fame,
Earning, she too, her praise
First in fiction, had since
Widen'd her sweep, and survey'd
History, politics, mind.[3]

WHAT TO READ ON THE WAY

Branwell's ill-judged letter to William Wordsworth and his later correspondence with Hartley Coleridge, Samuel Taylor Coleridge's eldest son. See Daphne du Maurier's *The Infernal World of Branwell Brontë* (London: Victor Gollancz, 1960), pp. 66–68.

William Wordsworth, *The Prelude* (1798).

Matthew Arnold, 'Haworth Parsonage, April 1855' (1856).

MANCHESTER

Plymouth Grove

Between 1851 and 1854, a year before she died, Charlotte visited her good friend and fellow author Elizabeth Gaskell three times at her home, 84 Plymouth Grove, Manchester. Gaskell lived here from 1850 to her death in 1865 and wrote several of her most famous books in the house, including *Cranford*, *North and South*, *Wives and Daughters*, and, of course, the biography of Charlotte. 84 Plymouth Grove is a grand Grade II* listed villa situated nearby to what is now the University of Manchester. The house played host to many eminent 19th-century thinkers, like Charles Dickens and John Ruskin, but it was Charlotte and Gaskell's friendship, and the resulting book, that went on to make the biggest impact by changing the way biographies were written and received. Through a £2.5m grant from the Heritage Lottery Fund, the house was opened to the public for the first time in 2014, offering a rare insight into Gaskell's life and the world of Victorian Manchester.

Victoria Bridge, Manchester, built 1837–39.

Mount Pleasant (Boundary Street West)

Patrick Brontë's eyes had been failing for some time before he was accompanied by Charlotte to Manchester for a cataract operation. The operation was successful, but they had to remain in the city for almost a month in order for the oculist to decipher whether the procedure had been successful. This involved sitting in a darkened room for most of the time. They stayed at 83 Mount Pleasant, which is now 59 Boundary Street West. It was here – in between seeing to her father and attempting to organise food for the two of them – that Charlotte began to write her most enduring novel, *Jane Eyre*. A blue plaque now marks the place where they stayed during August and September 1846, one year before the publication of *Jane Eyre*.

WHAT TO READ ON THE WAY

Elizabeth Gaskell's *North and South* (1854). A novel that contrasts the romanticised South with the industrialised North (I also recommend watching the 2004 BBC adaptation with Richard Armitage and Daniela Denby-Ashe – just because…).

Charlotte's *Jane Eyre* (1847); she started it in Manchester.

DERBYSHIRE

Hathersage

Charlotte visited Hathersage on a couple of occasions to visit Ellen, as her brother, the Reverend Henry Nussey, was the vicar there. Charlotte's interactions with Henry – who once proposed unsuccessfully to her and later considered becoming a missionary – most likely led to her composition of the poem 'The Missionary' and perhaps influenced the St John Rivers storyline of *Jane Eyre*. The village and its local vicinity had a major impact on Charlotte's most famous novel: the heroine shares a surname with the Eyre family who owned North Lees Hall, two miles outside of Hathersage and a prototype of Rochester's Thornfield Hall; and the village itself became Morton, where Jane's cousins live.

SOUTHERN ENGLAND

London

Charlotte made several visits to the city. First, on her way to Brussels in 1842, she stayed with her father and Emily in the Chapter Coffee House in Paternoster Row, which used to be an 18th-century literary scene hangout and became a gentleman's club for scholars like Patrick. She returned to London when her own literary career took off, often staying with her publisher George Smith in Gloucester Terrace, Hyde Park Gardens. Despite experiencing debilitating nerves and headaches during her trips, Charlotte made the most of her time in London: she took a tour of the Houses of Parliament, went round the Great Exhibition of 1851 five times, saw famous actors in Shakespearean plays, and met one of her favourite writers, William Thackeray.

St John's College, Cambridge

In October 1802, Patrick Brontë enrolled at St John's College, Cambridge, where he studied theology. At twenty-five, he was older than most of his peers by about ten years and, as an Irishman with a farming background, would have stood out from the crowd of young publicly educated boys. It was here, at St John's College, that Patrick altered his birth name (sometimes spelled as 'Brunty', sometimes as 'Prunty') to 'Brontë', which means 'thunder' in Greek. The college is one of the biggest in Cambridge and fellows of St John's are the only people except the royal family allowed to eat swan – although, there is no evidence to suggest Patrick tried the delicacy…

WHAT TO READ ON THE WAY

John Lock's *A Man of Sorrow: The Life, Letters and Times of the Rev. Patrick Brontë, 1777–1861* (1965).

William Makepeace Thackeray, *Vanity Fair* (1847–48).

St John's College.

A romantic depiction of Abbotsford House, near Melrose.

SCOTLAND

Abbotsford

Situated near Melrose in the Scottish Borders, this lavish residence was home to Sir Walter Scott, who, as we saw in the chapter on magic and the supernatural, was one of Charlotte's favourite authors. Charlotte and her publisher, George Smith (with whom she had a very close relationship), visited the property on 5 July 1850. If you're lucky, you can see her signature in the visitors' book, a tangible memento of her time there. Explore the house's beautiful gardens and even treat yourself to a stay in its Hope Scott Wing, where you can live like Sir Walter for a night.

WHAT TO READ ON THE WAY

Walter Scott's *The Black Dwarf* (1816) or *The Monastery* (1820), both set in the Scottish Borders.

Charlotte Brontë's *The Green Dwarf* (1833).

REPUBLIC OF IRELAND

Banagher, County Offaly

Originally born in Killead, County Antrim, Northern Ireland, Arthur Bell Nicholls grew up from the age of seven with his aunt and uncle in Banagher, King's County (now County Offaly). His uncle was the headmaster at the Royal School, which also doubled up as their family home, Cuba House. Charlotte and Arthur spent their honeymoon with his family in Banagher. To Margaret Wooler, Charlotte wrote: 'I cannot help feeling singularly interested in all about the place. In this house Mr. Nicholls was brought up by his uncle Dr. Bell. It is very large and looks externally like a gentleman's country-seat. Within, most of the rooms are lofty and spacious and some, the drawing room, dining room, etc. handsomely and commodiously furnished. The passages look desolate and bare. Our bedroom, a great room on the ground-floor would have looked gloomy when we were shewn into it but for the turf-fire that was burning in the wide old chimney.'[4] Sadly, the house, after extensive damage over the years, was demolished in the 1980s.

Charlotte and Arthur's honeymoon house at Banagher.

Drumballyroney, County Down

Patrick Brontë was born in Emdale, Drumballyroney, on St Patrick's Day, 17 March 1777. He was from a farming family, but Patrick took a different course in life to that of his siblings. Before attending St John's College, Cambridge, he founded his own school at the age of just sixteen. At Drumballyroney, there is now a Brontë Homeland Centre and a Brontë Homeland Drive, where you can trace the early life of Charlotte's father: it includes Drumballyroney Church and School where Patrick taught, preached and worshipped. You can also visit the child-hood home of Alice McClory, Patrick's mother and Charlotte's grandmother, on Brontë Road. If you fancy a more immersive experience, you can take a Brontë Homeland living history tour and meet 'Patrick' himself.

WHAT TO READ ON THE WAY

Patrick Brontë's *Cottage Poems*, published in 1811.

BRUSSELS

Quartier Isabelle

The Pensionnat Heger-Parent – where Charlotte and Emily studied and worked in 1842 and 1843 – was situated in this area on the Rue d'Isabelle, but sadly the majority of the Quartier Isabelle was destroyed in 1909. Nearby, on the Rue Terarken, there is an unofficial blue plaque commissioned by the Brontë Society. It reads: 'This plaque commemorates the old Quartier Isabelle of which the Rue Terarken is a lucky survival. Charlotte and Emily Brontë would have passed this street when going to the Pensionnat Heger in 1842–43. The memory of this area lives on in the vivid image Charlotte portrays in her novel *Villette*'.

Belliard Steps

In order to reach the Pensionnat Heger-Parent, the sisters had to walk down these steep stairs. The school was just across the road. When leaving the school and climbing back up the steps, a statue of General Belliard would have greeted the sisters and still greets walkers today. Charlotte and Emily, with their early interest in battles and bloodshed (particularly relating to the French Revolution and Napoleon Bonaparte), may have taken a shine to Belliard's statue: as an officer under Napoleon, he took part in the Egyptian campaign of 1798–1801 and was given the task of telling Napoleon of the surrender of Paris in 1814. Although the area has changed considerably since the two young Yorkshire women lived there, you can pay your respects to Belliard's memory and retrace the Brontës' steps by visiting the stairs and statue.

Parc de Bruxelles

When Lucy Snowe arrives in *Villette* (the fictionalised Brussels of Charlotte's third published novel), she is guided through this park late at night by an unknown gentleman as she tries to find her lodgings. Later in the novel, the park reappears when Lucy, under the influence of an opiate that was meant to send her to sleep but instead stimulates her, wanders through the city like a somnambulist during a night-time festival. She comes across a bandstand in the park in which a concert is being played. Built in 1841, the bandstand would have been seen by Charlotte during her she stay in Brussels, and it can still be visited today.

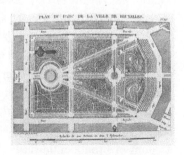

Parc de Bruxelles - plan.

St Michael and St Gudula Cathedral

Despite her deep dislike of Catholicism, Charlotte found this cathedral an appealing presence while living in Brussels; she visited it one evening during the summer of 1843, a time when she felt acutely lonely and on the brink of a nervous breakdown. This visit was immortalised in *Villette* when Lucy Snowe's alienation drives her to seek confession with a priest: 'It was an old solemn church, its pervading gloom not gilded but purpled by light shed through stained glass.'[5] The cathedral's exterior is grand and Gothic, a perfect fit for Charlotte's supernatural novel.

Chapelle Royal

During their time in the city, Charlotte and Emily worshipped here every Sunday. Situated in the Place du Musée, it has been recognised as the Protestant Church of Brussels (the Église Protestante de Bruxelles) since 1830, but King Leopold I of Belgium then gave it an alternative name of the Royal Chapel, as he worshipped here. The building itself has a wonderfully opulent marble interior and looks like the kind of beautifully detailed meringue-covered cake that would make any *Great British Bake Off* finalist proud.

WHAT TO READ ON THE WAY

Charlotte's *Villette* (1853). Deeply psychological, this novel walks the line between fantasy and realism.

Charlotte's *The Professor* (1857). Written in 1846, but published posthumously, this short work anticipates several themes that appear in Charlotte's later published writing, including education, tyranny and sexuality.

Helen MacEwan's *Down the Belliard Steps: Discovering the Brontës in Brussels* (Brussels Brontë Editions, 2012). An account of Brontë enthusiasts tracking Charlotte and Emily's time in Brussels.

NOTES & REFERENCES

Introduction

1. Charlotte Brontë to George Smith, 30 October 1852, in *Selected Letters of Charlotte Brontë*, ed. Margaret Smith (Oxford: Oxford University Press, 2010), pp. 207–208.

Chapter One: The Life and Works of Charlotte

1. Admissions register of the Clergy Daughters' School, Cowan Bridge, 1824–39, in *The Brontës: A Life in Letters*, ed. Juliet Barker (London: Viking, 1997), p. 7.
2. Charlotte Brontë, *Jane Eyre*, ed. Stevie Davies (London: Penguin Classics, 2006), p. 71.
3. See Juliet Barker, *The Brontës*, (London: Phoenix, 1995), p. 181.
4. Charlotte Brontë, 'Roe Head Journal Fragments [2]', in *Tales of Angria*, ed. Heather Glen (London: Penguin Classics, 2006), p. 453.
5. Charlotte Brontë, 'Roe Head Journal Fragments [4]', in The Brontës, *Tales of Glass Town, Angria, and Gondal: Selected Writings*, ed. Christine Alexander (Oxford: Oxford University Press, 2010), p. 165.
6. Charlotte Brontë, 'Farewell to Angria', in The Brontës, *Tales of Glass Town, Angria, and Gondal: Selected Writings*, p. 314.
7. Charlotte to Emily, 8 June 1839, in *The Brontës: A Life in Letters*, pp. 64–65.
8. Charlotte to Ellen Nussey, Brussels, 13 October 1843, in *The Brontës: A Life in Letters*, p. 118.
9. Charlotte to Ellen, Haworth, 23 January 1844, in *The Brontës: A Life in Letters*, p. 119. In the mid-19th century, the term 'disinterested' was commonly used to refer to a lack of selfish motive, not simply a lack of general interest. In this instance, it is unclear as to which definition Charlotte was referring.
10. Charlotte to Monsieur Héger, Haworth, 24 July 1844, in *The Brontës: A Life in Letters*, p. 121.
11. Charlotte Brontë, 'Biographical Notice of Ellis and Acton Bell, 1850', in *The Brontës: A Life in Letters*, p. 140.
12. *Ibid*, p. 141.
13. Although, as Lucasta Miller notes, this was perhaps not their first foray into publication, as there is evidence that Charlotte and Anne had had some success in publishing a few pieces anonymously. See Lucasta Miller, *The Brontë Myth*, (London: Vintage, 2002), p. 11.
14. See Heather Glen's notes in Charlotte Brontë, *The Professor*, (London: Penguin Classics, 2003), p. 303.
15. Charlotte to Smith, Elder & Co., 12 September 1847, in *The Brontës: A Life in Letters*, p. 165.
16. Charlotte to Ellen, 15 May 1840, in *The Brontës: A Life in Letters*, p. 75.
17. Charlotte to Ellen, 12 March 1839, in *Selected Letters of Charlotte Brontë*, p. 11.
18. Virginia Woolf, 'Jane Eyre and Wuthering Heights', *The Common Reader* (London: Hogarth Press, 1951), pp. 196–204, p. 198.
19. Charlotte to Ellen, 4 August 1839, in *The Brontës: A Life in Letters*, p. 67. The spelling of David Bryce's surname varies; some scholars, such as Lyndall Gordon and older sources, use 'Bryce', whereas others, such as Juliet Barker, use 'Pryce'. Although

Charlotte herself clearly chose to call him 'Mr. Price', I enjoy the confusion surrounding his name, as it reminds me of Patrick Brontë's own 'Prunty/ Brunty' dilemma. For this reason, I have used 'Bryce' and juxtaposed this with Charlotte's own use of 'Price', to highlight the slipperiness of names at this time.

20. *Ibid*, p. 68.

21. Juliet Barker, *The Brontës*, p. 326.

22. Charlotte to Ellen, 15 May 1840, in *The Brontës: A Life in Letters*, p. 76.

23. Charlotte to Monsieur Héger, 8 January 1845, in *The Brontës: A Life in Letters*, pp. 124–125.

24. Charlotte to Monsieur Héger, 18 November 1845, in *The Brontës: A Life in Letters*, pp. 138–139.

25. See Juliet Barker, *The Brontës*, p. 669.

26. William Makepeace Thackeray to Lucy Baxter, 11 March 1853, in *The Brontës: The Critical Heritage*, ed. Miriam Allott (London: Routledge & Kegan Paul, 1974), pp. 196–197.

27. Charlotte to Ellen, 11 April 1854, in *Selected Letters of Charlotte Brontë*, pp. 227–228.

28. Charlotte to Ellen, 20 October 1854, in *The Brontës: A Life in Letters*, p. 394.

29. Charlotte to Ellen, 26 December 1854, in *The Brontës: A Life in Letters*, p. 396.

30. Charlotte to W.S. Williams, 2 October 1848, in *Selected Letters of Charlotte Brontë*, p. 120.

31. Robert Edric, *Sanctuary*, (London: Black Swan, 2015).

32. Charlotte to W.S. Williams, 2 October 1848, in *Selected Letters of Charlotte Brontë*, p. 121.

33. Daphne du Maurier, *The Infernal World of Branwell Brontë*, (London: Virago, 2006).

34. Elizabeth Gaskell, *The Life of Charlotte Brontë*, ed. Alan Shelston, (Middlesex: Penguin Books, 1977), p. 356.

35. Charlotte to W.S. Williams, 25 December 1848, in *Selected Letters of Charlotte Brontë*, pp. 128–129.

36. See Juliet Barker, *The Brontës*, p. 579.

37. Anne to Ellen, 5 April 1849, in *The Brontës: A Life in Letters*, p. 229.

38. Charlotte to W.S. Williams, 4 June 1849, in *The Brontës: A Life in Letters*, pp. 236–237.

39. Charlotte Brontë, *Shirley*, ed. Jessica Cox (London: Penguin Classics, 2006), p. 392.

40. Robert Southey quotes from Charlotte's letter to him: 'You who so ardently desire "to be for ever known" as a poetess'. See Robert Southey to Charlotte Brontë, 12 March 1837, in *The Letters of Charlotte Brontë: With a Selection of Letters from Family and Friends: Volume I: 1829–1847*, ed. Margaret Smith (Oxford: Oxford University Press, 1995), p. 166.

41. See Juliet Barker, *The Brontës*, p. 610.

42. See Juliet Barker, *The Brontës*, p. 643.

43. See Lucasta Miller, *The Brontë Myth*.

44. Charlotte to George Smith, 26 March 1853, in *Selected Letters of Charlotte*

Brontë, pp. 217–218.

45. Charlotte to Ellen, [?]24 September 1849, in *Selected Letters of Charlotte Brontë*, p. 145.

Chapter Two: Charlotte's Afterlives

1. Charlotte Brontë, 'Editor's Preface to the New [1850] Edition of *Wuthering Heights*', in Emily Brontë, *Wuthering Heights*, ed. Pauline Nestor (London: Penguin Classics, 2003), l–liv, p. lii.

2. Charlotte Brontë, 'Biographical Notice of Ellis and Acton Bell', in Emily Brontë, *Wuthering Heights*, xliii – xlix, p. xlvii.

3. Barbara Mitchell, 'The Biographical Process: Writing the Lives of Charlotte Brontë', Ph.D Thesis, The University of Leeds (December 1994). See also Lucasta Miller, *The Brontë Myth*.

4. Charlotte Brontë, 'Editor's Preface to the New [1850] Edition of *Wuthering Heights*', p. l.

5. *Ibid*, p. li.

6. Ted Hughes, 'Haworth Parsonage', *Remains of Elmet*, (London: Faber & Faber, 2011).

7. Harriet Martineau, 'Obituary of Charlotte Brontë', *Daily News*, April 1855, in *The Brontës: The Critical Heritage*, pp. 301–304.

8. *Ibid*, p. 304.

9. Elizabeth Gaskell, *The Life of Charlotte Brontë*, p. 89.

10. *Ibid*, p. 90.

11. *Ibid*, p. 526.

12. *Ibid*.

13. See Fannie E. Ratchford, *The Brontës' Web of Childhood*, (New York: Columbia University Press, 1941). And see ed. T.J. Wise and J.A. Symington, *The Brontës, Their Lives, Friendships and Correspondence*, (Oxford: Blackwell, 1932).

14. Winifred Gérin, *Charlotte Brontë: The Evolution of Genius* (Oxford: Oxford University Press, 1977), p. xiv.

15. Virginia Woolf, 'The Art of Biography', *Selected Essays*, ed. David Bradshaw (Oxford: Oxford World's Classics, 2008), pp. 116–123.

16. Barbara Hardy, 'Review: Winifred Gérin, *Charlotte Brontë: The Evolution of Genius*', *Nineteenth-Century Fiction*, 23/2 (1968), pp. 240–243, p. 242.

17. Lyndall Gordon, *Charlotte Brontë: A Passionate Life*, (London: Chatto & Windus, 1994), p. 4.

18. Paula Byrne, 'Sex, Drugs and Charlotte Brontë', *The Times*, 24 October 2015.

19. Mark Bostridge, 'Charlotte Brontë: Cinderella or Ugly Sister?', *The Spectator*, 24 October 2015.

20. Claire Harman, *Charlotte Brontë: A Life* (London: Viking, 2015), pp. 178–179.

21. *Ibid*, p. 5.

22. Sally Wainwright, '*To Walk Invisible*: Sally Wainwright's drama looks anew at the extraordinary Brontë family', BBC Media Centre, 8 December 2016, www.bbc.co.uk/mediacentre/mediapacks/towalk.

23. Siv Jansson, '"Their Name Was Brontë": Brontë Biography on Screen', *Brontë*

Studies, 43/1 (2018), pp. 32–40, p. 39.

24. 'Could photograph be of Brontë sisters?', *The Telegraph and Argus*, 13 March 2012, www.thetelegraphandargus.co.uk/news/9587270. Could_photograph_be_of_Bronte_sisters_/.

25. *Ibid.*

26. Amber K. Regis and Deborah Wynne, 'Introduction: Picturing Charlotte Brontë', in *Charlotte Brontë: Legacies and Afterlives*, eds. Regis and Wynne, (Manchester: Manchester University Press, 2017), pp. 1–39, p. 10.

27. *Ibid.*

28. *Ibid.*

29. Patrick Brontë to George Smith, 2 August 1850, in *The Letters of Charlotte Brontë: With a Selection of Letters from Family and Friends: Volume II: 1848–1851*, ed. Margaret Smith, (Oxford: Oxford University Press, 2000), p. 435.

30. *Ibid*, p. 16.

31. Alice Spawls, 'If It Weren't for Charlotte', *London Review of Books*, 39/22 (November 2017).

32. *Ibid.*

33. Following the publication of *Jane Eyre*, Charlotte wrote to W. S. Williams: 'What author would be without the advantage of being able to walk invisible?' See Charlotte Brontë to W. S. Williams, 4 January 1848, in *The Letters of Charlotte Brontë: Volume II: 1848–1851*, p. 4.

34. Elizabeth Gaskell, *The Life of Charlotte Brontë*, p. 308.

35. *Ibid.*

36. Cora Kaplan, 'Heroines, Hysteria and History: Jane Eyre and her Critics', in *Victoriana: Histories, Fictions Criticism* (Edinburgh: Edinburgh University Press, 2007), p. 31.

37. Laurent Bury, 'Creative (mis)reading? Paula Rego's *Jane Eyre*', *Revue LISA*, 7/4 (2009), pp. 166–178.

38. Marina Warner, 'An Artist's Dream', *Tate*, December 2003.

39. Cora Kaplan, 'Heroines, Hysteria and History: Jane Eyre and her Critics', p. 33.

40. Sally Cookson, 'Jane Eyre, feminist icon', *Standard Issue*, 29 September 2015.

41. Susannah Clapp, 'Jane Eyre review – aflame with passion and madness', *The Guardian*, 27 September 2015.

42. Sandra Gilbert and Susan Guber, *The Madwoman in the Attic: The Woman Writer and the Nineteenth-Century Literary Imagination* (London: Yale University Press, 2000), p. 347.

43. Eleanor Turney, 'Interview with Sally Cookson: Get the Golden Axe Out and Kill Your Darlings', *Exeunt Magazine*, 14 September 2015.

Chapter Three: Charlotte in Nature

1. Charlotte Brontë, *Shirley*, p.60.

2. See the Public Health Act (11 & 12 Vict., cap. 63). Report at www.bl.uk/ collection-items/sanitary-report-on-haworth-home-to-the-bronts

3. Juliet Barker, *The Brontës*, p. 92.

4. See also Lucasta Miller, *The Brontë Myth*.

5. Elizabeth Gaskell, *The Life of Charlotte Brontë*, pp. 55–56.

6. Charlotte Brontë, *The Professor*, p.172.

7. Patrick Branwell Brontë to William Wordsworth, 19 January 1837, in *The Brontës: Their Lives, Friendships & Correspondence in Four Volumes: Vol I: 1777–1843*, eds. T.J. Wise and J.A. Symington (Oxford: Blackwell, 1932), pp. 151–152.

8. Robert Southey to Charlotte Brontë, March 1837, in *The Brontës: A Life in Letters*, pp. 46–48.

9. Lord Byron, 'Childe Harold's Pilgrimage', Canto III, LXXI–LXXII, *Selected Poems*, eds. Susan J. Wolfson and Peter J. Manning (London: Penguin, 2005), pp. 439–440.

10. William Wordsworth's 'Lines Written a Few Miles above Tintern Abbey, 1798', *The Major Works*, ed. Stephen Gill (Oxford: Oxford World's Classics, 2008), pp. 131–135, pp. 134–135.

11. Charlotte Brontë, *Shirley*, p.16.

12. Elizabeth Gaskell, *The Life of Charlotte Brontë*, p. 507.

13. Charlotte to Ellen, 4 July 1834, *Selected Letters of Charlotte Brontë*, pp. 4–5.

14. Charlotte Brontë, *Jane Eyre*, pp. 10–11.

15. Charlotte Brontë, *Jane Eyre*, p. 129.

16. Charlotte to Reverend Patrick Brontë, 7 June 1851, *The Letters of Charlotte Brontë: With a Selection of Letters from Family and Friends: Vol II: 1848–1851*, ed. Margaret Smith (Oxford: Oxford University Press, 2000), pp. 630–631, p. 630.

17. Elizabeth Gaskell, *The Life of Charlotte Brontë*, p. 418.

18. Charlotte Brontë, *Jane Eyre*, pp. 90–91.

19. Charlotte Brontë, *Jane Eyre*, p. 90.

Chapter Four: Magical Charlotte

1. Charlotte to George Henry Lewes, 12 January 1848, in *Selected Letters of Charlotte Brontë*, pp. 98–99.

2. See Christine Alexander's Introduction in The Brontës, *Tales of Glass Town, Angria, and Gondal: Selected Writings*.

3. Charlotte Brontë, 'The History of the Year', 12 March 1829, in The Brontës, *Tales of Glass Town, Angria, and Gondal: Selected Writings*, p. 3.

4. Charlotte Brontë, 'The Twelve Adventurers', 15 April 1829, in The Brontës, *Tales of Glass Town, Angria, and Gondal: Selected Writings*, pp. 5–15, p. 8.

5. Susan Carlson, 'Fantasies of Death and Violence in the Early Juvenilia of Charlotte Brontë (1829–32)', *Brontë Studies*, 1 July 2002, 27/2, pp. 101–111.

6. Although, it has to be said that Branwell wasn't a big fan of the tyranny of the Chief Genii and he incited a revolt against them.

7. Charlotte *Brontë*, 'Sir – it is well known that the Genii', in *The Early Writings of Charlotte Brontë: 1826–1832*, ed. Christine Alexander (Oxford: Blackwell, 1987), p. 39.

8. Charlotte Brontë, 'The trumpet hath sounded', 11 December 1831, in *The Poems of Charlotte Brontë*, ed. Tom Winnifrith (Oxford: Blackwell, 1984), pp. 133–135, p.134.

9. Charlotte Brontë, *Jane Eyre*, p. 132.

10. Charlotte Brontë, *Jane Eyre*, p. 144.

11. Charlotte Brontë, *Jane Eyre*, pp. 16–17.

12. Charlotte Brontë, *Jane Eyre*, pp. 20–21.

13. John Sutherland, 'Can Jane Eyre Be Happy?', *Can Jane Eyre Be Happy? More Puzzles in Classic Fiction* (Oxford: Oxford University Press, 2001), pp. 68–80.

14. Charlotte Brontë, *Jane Eyre*, pp. 338–339.

15. William Makepeace Thackeray to W.S. Williams, 23 October 1847, in *The Letters and Private Papers of W.M. Thackeray: Vol II: 1841–1851*, ed. Gordon N. Ray (London: Oxford University Press, 1945), pp. 318–319, p. 319.

16. Charlotte Brontë, *Villette, eds.* Margaret Smith and Herbert Rosengarten (Oxford: Oxford World's Classics, 2008), pp. 106–107.

17. Charlotte Brontë, *Villette*, pp. 296–297.

18. Christopher Schobert, 'Guillermo del Toro's 'Crimson Peak' is a delicious Bronte stew', *The Buffalo News*, 10 October 2015.

Chapter Five: Charlotte and Ideology

1. Charlotte Brontë, *Shirley*, p. 598.

2. Charlotte Brontë, 'The History of the Year', 12 March 1829, in The Brontës, *Tales of Glass Town, Angria, and Gondal: Selected Writings*, p. 3.

3. Patricia Ingham, *The Brontës: Authors in Context*, (Oxford: Oxford University Press, 2008), pp. 40–41.

4. Samuel Johnson, 'Tory', *A Dictionary of the English Language: in which the words are deduced from their originals, and illustrated in their different significations by examples from the best writers. To which are prefixed, a history of the language, and an English grammar* (London: Times Books Ltd., 1979).

5. Elizabeth Gaskell, *The Life of Charlotte Brontë*, p. 131.

6. Charlotte to George Smith, 14 February 1852, in *Selected Letters*, pp. 198–199.

7. Charlotte to Margaret Wooler, 31 March 1848, in *The Letters of Charlotte Brontë: With a Selection of Letters from Family and Friends: Volume II: 1848– 1851*, pp. 47–49, p. 48.

8. Charlotte to W.S. Williams, 20 April 1848, in *The Letters of Charlotte Brontë: Volume II*, pp. 51–52.

9. See Terry Eagleton, *Myths of Power: A Marxist Study of the Brontës*, (Basingstoke: Macmillan, 1988); Philip Rogers, 'Tory Brontë: *Shirley* and the 'MAN', *Nineteenth-Century Literature*, 58/2 (2003), pp. 141–175; and Lucasta Miller's Introduction in *Shirley*, pp. xi–xxxiv.

10. Charlotte Brontë, *Shirley*, pp. 327–328.

11. Robert Southey to Charlotte, 12 March 1837, in *The Letters of Charlotte Brontë: Volume I*, pp. 165–168.

12. Charlotte Brontë, *Shirley*, p. 333.
13. Charlotte Brontë, *Shirley*, pp. 369–371.
14. Emma Thompson, Academy Awards acceptance speech, 25 March 1996.
15. Mary Taylor to Charlotte, *The Letters of Charlotte Brontë: Vol. II*, p. 392.
16. Charlotte Brontë, *Jane Eyre*, p. 338.
17. Charlotte Brontë, *Jane Eyre*, p. 337.
18. Charlotte Brontë, *Jane Eyre*, p. 347.
19. Chimamanda Ngozi Adichie, 'We Should All Be Feminists', 12 April 2013.
20. Beyoncé, '***Flawless', feat. Chimamanda Ngozi Adichie.
21. See, for example, Terry Eagleton, *Myths of Power*, p. 29.
22. Elaine Showalter, 'Charlotte Brontë: Feminine Heroine', in *Jane Eyre*, ed. Heather Glen (Basingstoke: Macmillan, 1997), p.70.
23. For an insight into this undercurrent of violence, see Heather Glen's Introduction in *The Professor*, pp. 7–31.
24. Charlotte Brontë, *Jane Eyre*, p. 310.
25. See Edwin Percy Whipple, 'Novels of the Season', *North American Review*, 67/141 (October 1848), p. 357.
26. Charlotte Brontë, *Jane Eyre*, p. 363.
27. Charlotte Brontë, *Jane Eyre*, pp. 129–130.
28. Charlotte Brontë, *Jane Eyre*, p. 292.
29. Charlotte Brontë, *Jane Eyre*, p. 293.

Chapter Six: (Desperately) Seeking Charlotte

1. Charlotte to Ellen Nussey, 6 June 1852, in *The Brontës: A Life in Letters*, p. 349.
2. Charlotte Brontë, *Shirley*, p. 141.
3. Matthew Arnold, 'Haworth Churchyard', *Poems* (London: J.M. Dent & Sons Ltd., 1948), pp. 234–237, p. 234.
4. Charlotte to Margaret Wooler, 10 July 1854, *The Letters of Charlotte Brontë: Vol III: 1852–1855*, 275–278, p. 276.
5. Charlotte Brontë, *Villette*, p. 161.

SELECTED BIBLIOGRAPHY

Charlotte Brontë, *Jane Eyre*, ed. Stevie Davies (London: Penguin Classics, 2006).

The Professor, ed. Heather Glen (London: Penguin Classics, 1989).

Shirley, ed. Jessica Cox (London: Penguin Classics, 2006).

Villette, ed. Margaret Smith and Herbert Rosengarten (Oxford: Oxford World's Classics, 2008).

Tales of Angria, ed. Heather Glen (London: Penguin Classics, 2006).

The Brontës, *Tales of Glass Town, Angria, and Gondal: Selected Writings*, ed. Christine Alexander (Oxford: Oxford World's Classics, 2010).

Elizabeth Gaskell, *The Life of Charlotte Brontë* (Middlesex: Penguin Books, 1977)

T.J. Wise and J.A. Symington, *The Brontës, Their Lives, Friendships and Correspondence in Four Volumes* (Oxford: Blackwell, 1932).

The Brontës: The Critical Heritage, ed. Miriam Allott (London: Routledge & Kegan Paul, 1974).

The Brontës: A Life in Letters, ed. Juliet Barker (London: Viking, 1997).

The Letters of Charlotte Brontë: With a Selection of Letters from Family and Friends: Volume I: 1829–1847, ed. Margaret Smith (Oxford: Oxford University Press, 1995).

The Letters of Charlotte Brontë: With a Selection of Letters from Family and Friends: Volume II: 1848–1851, ed. Margaret Smith (Oxford: Oxford University Press, 2000).

The Letters of Charlotte Brontë: With a Selection of Letters from Family and Friends: Volume III: 1852–1855, ed. Margaret Smith (Oxford: Oxford University Press, 2004).

Selected Letters of Charlotte Brontë, ed. Margaret Smith (Oxford: Oxford University Press, 2010).

Selected Bibliography

* * *

Juliet Barker, *The Brontës* (London: Phoenix, 1995).

Susan Carlson, 'Fantasies of Death and Violence in the Early Juvenilia of Charlotte Brontë (1829–32)', *Brontë Studies*, 1 July 2002, 27/2, pp. 101–111.

Terry Eagleton, *Myths of Power: A Marxist Study of the Brontës* (Basingstoke: Macmillan, 1988).

Rebecca Fraser, *Charlotte Brontë: A Writer's Life* (London: Vintage, 2015).

Sarah Freeman, *Brontë in Love* (Ilkley: Great Northern Books, 2010).

Winifred Gérin, *Charlotte Brontë: The Evolution of Genius* (Oxford: Oxford University Press, 1977).

Sandra Gilbert and Susan Guber, *The Madwoman in the Attic: The Woman Writer and the Nineteenth-Century Literary Imagination* (London: Yale University Press, 2000).

Lyndall Gordon, *Charlotte Brontë: A Passionate Life* (London: Virago, 2008).

Claire Harman, *Charlotte Brontë: A Life* (London: Viking, 2015).

Patricia Ingham, *The Brontës: Authors in Context* (Oxford: Oxford University Press, 2008).

Sara Lodge, *Charlotte Brontë: Jane Eyre* (Houndmills: Palgrave Macmillan, 2009).

Lucasta Miller, *The Brontë Myth* (London: Jonathan Cape, 2001).

Fannie E. Ratchford, *The Brontës' Web of Childhood* (New York: Columbia University Press, 1941).

Paula Rego, *Paula Rego: Jane Eyre and Other Stories* (London: Marlborough Fine Art, c.2003).

John Sutherland, *Can Jane Eyre Be Happy? More Puzzles in Classic Fiction* (Oxford: Oxford University Press, 2001).

Virginia Woolf, 'The Art of Biography', *Selected Essays*, ed. David Bradshaw (Oxford: Oxford World's Classics, 2008), pp. 116–123.

ACKNOWLEDGEMENTS

I'm incredibly grateful to Sara Hunt, who first conceived of the idea for this book and gave me the wonderful opportunity to write it. I'm also very thankful for Craig Hillsley's editing skills – without which, the chapters in this book may have ended up as a Brontë-inspired stream of consciousness. The Saraband team has made what could have been a daunting task feel fun, and for that I'm truly grateful. Special thanks also go to Bill Johncocks for preparing the index for this new edition. I also want to thank my friends and family for their endless support and love.

Finally, I want to dedicate this book to the best woman I know: my Mum, Anne Bush.

INDEX

Note: Italic page references indicate illustrations. The names of real people are inverted, as in 'Gaskell, Elizabeth', except where they are regularly referred to by given name only, as with 'Ellen (Nussey)': the names of fictional characters are not inverted (so 'Bertha Mason' at B; 'Jane Eyre' at J) unless their given names are not used, as in 'Rochester (Edward)'.

Hughes, Ted 3

DR SOPHIE FRANKLIN is a lecturer and researcher in the English department at Tübingen University, Germany. Her research specialises in nineteenth-century literature and culture, with expertise in representations of violence, the Brontës, and afterlives. She has taught at several institutions, including Nottingham  Trent University and the University of Newcastle. Sophie received her PhD from Durham University after receiving a First from St Andrews University. Alongside her academic career, she has co-organised Brontë conferences, worked at the Brontë Society, in bookselling, and as an editorial assistant for an independent publishing house.